OTHER BOOKS B

MW01166532

The Blessing Behind Closed Doors
Size Does Matter: Moving Your Ministry from Micro to Mega
Dr. R. A. Vernon's 10 Rules of Dating

HELP!
MY PASTOR'S
UNDER
PRESSURE!

HOW LEADERS CAN HELP THEIR PASTOR SUCCEED

R.A. VERNON

Copyright © 2017 by Dr. R. A. Vernon

All rights reserved. No part of this publication may be reproduced, stored in any retrieval system, or transmitted in any form by any means—electronic, mechanical, photocopy, recording, or otherwise—without prior written permission of the publisher, except as provided by United States of America copyright law.

All scriptures taken from the New American Standard Bible (NASB) except where indicated.

Copyright © 1960, 1962, 1963, 1968, 1971, 1972, 1973, 1975, 1977, 1995 by The Lockman Foundation Used by permission. www.lockman.org

Scripture quotations marked (MSG) or "The Message" are taken from The Message. Copyright 1993, 1994, 1995, 1996, 2000, 2001, 2002. Used by permission of NavPress Publishing Group. www.navpress.com

Scripture quotations marked (NLT) are taken from the Holy Bible, New Living Translation, copyright © 1996, 2004, 2007 by Tyndale House Foundation. Used by permission of Tyndale House Publishers, Inc., Carol Stream, Illinois 60188. All rights reserved.

Printed in the United States of America

Victory Media & Publishing
16781 Chagrin Boulevard #132
Cleveland, OH 44120

ISBN-13: 978099912300

DEDICATION

In my early thirties, pastors from across the nation and the world began coming to Cleveland seeking solutions and advice regarding pastoral ministry. So much so that my wife and I sensed a calling within a calling to begin speaking into the lives of pastors and their spouses and become a soft place for them to land. That eventually led to us launching our fellowship for Senior Pastors called The Shepherds Connection.

In a very real sense, it was my connection to them that birthed this work. While preparing for our Gathering of the Shepherds Pastors and Leaders Training one year, I decided to do something different. I allowed all the staff and leadership of the various ministries present to join their senior pastors in a joint session where I taught on the pressures of pastoring.

By the end of the session, many of the support staff were approaching their pastors in tears saying that had never considered the many pressures that they faced. It was at that moment that I knew it was my obligation to be a voice for senior pastors across the world who humbly and sincerely serve congregations who unknowingly take them for granted; not out of nefarious intentions, but because of a lack of knowledge.

To that end, this book is dedicated first and foremost to the staff, leadership, and faithful members of The Word Church. For nearly two decades you have made me feel like the most blessed pastor in the world. No pastor, including me, is exempt from all the pressures I discuss in this book, but you have made it so much easier for me with your love, loyalty, and financial support. You help feed and clothe my children and I will always love you for that.

I also dedicate this work to the best pastors' fellowship in the world—The Shepherds Connection. Pastors don't easily trust and submit themselves, their families, and their ministries to just anyone, and my wife and I never take that for granted.

Finally, this book is dedicated to the thousands of pastors across the world who unreservedly avail themselves to congregations, both large and small, and handsomely handle the many unavoidable pressures that come with pastoring. I pray this book in some way helps to relieve at least some of it.

TABLE OF CONTENTS

FOREWORD

No other professional faces more of the wear and tear of life than a pastor.

A doctor sees you for physical needs. An attorney sees you for legal needs. A banker sees you for financial needs. But a pastor sees you for all your needs. Not only that, he sees you in all your ages and stages of life.

He sees you when you're doing great as well as when you're not; when you're getting married and when you're getting divorced; when you get a new job and when you lose that job; when you're moving into a new house and when you're being evicted; when there are births and when there are deaths; when you're healthy and when you're in the hospital.

His life is a constant rollercoaster of emotions. Each phone call is about joy or heartache, hope or despair. Furthermore, a pastor is supposed to be able to fix any situation, have the greatest counsel, provide the necessary resources, and in so doing, keep everyone happy. The pastor is everyone's 911.

But, who's the pastor's 911? Who cares for him? Who encourages her? Where does your pastor go to be holistically replenished? Who's your pastor's pain partner?

You can be that pressure valve—that gift, in your pastor's life.

In this book, my friend Dr. R.A. Vernon unpacks these questions in a methodical and succinct manner. This book doesn't make the pastor feel like a victim, nor does it place a guilt trip on the members—it offers tangible hope and help.

This book will save pastors and their families from unnecessary pain, reenergize churches, and advance the Kingdom of our Lord.

Sam Chand
Leadership Consultant and Author of Leadership Pain

NOTE

Let me say at the outset that I am aware of the growing number of female senior pastors, and appreciate the receptiveness we've experienced as a body of believers to women in senior leadership positions.

Thus, while fully affirming women as spiritual leaders, to avoid having to switch back and forth between gender pronouns throughout, I will refer to the pastoral position in the masculine.

PREFACE

A mother went to wake her son for church one Sunday morning. When she knocked on his door, he said, "I'm not going!"

"Why not?" asked his mother.

"I'll give you two good reasons," he said. "One, they don't like me. Two, I don't like them."

His mother replied, "I'll give you two good reasons why YOU WILL go to church. One, you're 47 years old. Two, you're the pastor!"

Pastoring is not for the faint of heart. It is often isolating, demanding, and wholly taxing, encroaching on every aspect of your being—the physical, mental, emotional, and spiritual.

"One of you shall betray me...but until you do, I'm going to love, cover, and teach you everything I know."

I often joke with other pastors whom I train that every pastor should start his meetings this way, the way Jesus did at The Last Supper, appending that last clause to His declarative. Why? Because it's true.

Being betrayed by someone near and dear to our hearts is an imminent certainty.

The difference is, Jesus knew who His betrayer would be —we seldom do.

When Jesus uttered those words, a larger scheme of events ensued, leading up to the first and greatest martyrdom known to man.[1]

Pastors are still being slaughtered, however, modern-day martyrdom does not rival the physical suffering of first century persecution.

Our martyrdom, as it were, is social media and Internet assassination, where any person with access to an electronic device can destroy our character; where in a matter of hours, a rumor can annihilate both the life and ministry that took decades to build; it's the gut-wrenching ravages of rejection, betrayal, and disloyalty.

If you pastor long enough, someone you love, whom you've baptized, advised, hired, inspired, married, carried, taught, and fought for; someone whose baby you blessed, whose grandmother you prayed for, who you've bailed out and helped up, someone who you've done all you could for —will one day, without any notice, turn their back on you, and act as if you never did a thing for them.

This is the life of most pastors, and it is not an occasional happenstance; it is an occupational hazard. Even if he never mentions it to you, your pastor is always acutely aware of this reality.

At some point in their ministry, a pastor will be hurt by someone whom they've trusted. It's unfortunate, but inevitable.

This sobering reality makes many pastors want to encase their hearts in an impenetrable armor. The problem with this? If you guard your heart, it will never get broken, but it will stay cold. If you risk your heart, it will often get broken, but it will stay warm.

This is a double-edged sword if there ever was one.

It is impossible to love God's people with a cold heart. Not only can you not give love, you cannot receive it either. You're not likely to get hurt, but you'll never experience the fullness of life and love the way God intended.

Now, I'm at a point in my life and ministry where I can't get enough of love's splendor. I bask in it. From my deep awe of God's love for me, to the affection from my wife, to the adoration in my children's eyes when I catch them watching me, to the admiration I feel from my members, I fully immerse myself in it whenever I can.

On the other hand, I also embrace the pain, which I wasn't always able to do.

James 1:2-4 says:

> "[2]Consider it all joy, my brethren, when you encounter various trials, [3]knowing that the testing of your faith produces endurance. [4]And let endurance have its perfect result, so that you may be perfect and complete, lacking in nothing."

But Eugene Peterson's version of Romans 5:3-5 is the one that rejuvenates my spirit when I suffer a betrayal:

> "There's more to come: We continue to shout our praise even when we're hemmed in with troubles, because we know how troubles can develop passionate patience in us, and how that patience in turn forges the tempered steel of virtue, keeping us alert for whatever God will do next. In alert expectancy such as this, we're never left feeling shortchanged. Quite the contrary—we can't round up enough containers to hold everything God generously pours into our lives through the Holy Spirit!"

So, no, I don't like being hurt, but I am "never left feeling shortchanged." It is always better on the other side.

Still, this is the incredible risk and reward of leadership. We are forced to do our jobs daily and function like we won't get hurt, knowing full well we will be, suffer through it, and wait patiently for the time to come when we can count ourselves better for it.

This is also the paradox of pastoring.

It is the only job in the world that I would neither trade, nor recommend, unless you are built for everything I just described and more.

In addition, there are pressures, pressures that come with the call, pressures that are substantially more affective than those experienced by the average person just doing their job.

And this brings us to the beginning of my case.

I am madly in love with Jesus.

It is in Him that I live, move, and have my being. He is the reason I exist and everything—and I do mean everything—that I have and have accomplished is because of His grace and favor; I am nothing without Him and forever in awe of His power. He is my refuge and my strength, my best friend and my Father, and my purpose in life is to bring Him glory.

As a Christian, you undoubtedly identify with most if not all of what you just read, and not only that, my words probably resonated deep in your spirit.

Though I could've assumed it a given, I led with my deference to our Savior because from here on out, the tone of this book is frank, my tone firm, my argument forward... and it's not about Jesus.

In case you didn't notice from the title, it's about your pastor.

If you're looking for a book about Jesus, however, there's this great book—the bestselling book of all time in fact—that you might want to pick up. It's called *The Holy Bible*, readily available at your favorite bookseller.

Now, while this book isn't about Jesus, He did tell me to write it.

Why?

Because the reality in the Judeo-Christian Church is that while we realize, respect, and revere the person and authority of Jesus Christ, the same rationale that informs this understanding is conspicuously missing when it comes to the lay pastor's relational rank relative to his membership, or those under his spiritual covering.

In other words, we know who Jesus is, but we don't know who the pastor is.

I say this experientially. I have nearly two decades of pastoring behind me, and today, I lead a wonderful church where in the last seventeen years, I have seldom encountered any form of dishonor, even in tense or otherwise uncomfortable situations.

The formative years of my pastoral career were not as forgiving. I endured more disrespect and insolence during that time than ever before or since. Teenagers would stand up in meetings and tell me what they thought about me based on what they'd heard their parents say.

Ultimately, things got so bad that one Sunday morning, the leaders of the church locked me—and several hundred others—out, refusing to allow me to baptize a dozen or so new converts nor permitting us to worship that day...yeah, it was bad.

To be fair, there were myriad factors at work during my first pastoral tenure that contributed to my eventual ousting—not the least of which was God posturing me for something far more apropos considering my visionary leadership style.

Prior to my election, for years, the church rehearsed rigid routines and held fast to habits that had been hemmed into their heritage. These they trusted far more than the young, fly, inexperienced rookie they had just voted in, who tried to homogenize old-school values with modern-day means.

But what you read at present is in my hindsight. That's not what I knew nor how I felt back then. Back then, it was all pain. Enervating, exhausting, exasperating, pain. Pain that I had not yet learned to embrace.

Reflection, introspection, years of laborious emotional work, and spiritual maturity caused me to realize that I could have done more to consider how my leadership style would affect those who I had been called to cover. Had I been more cognizant, I could've been more considerate of how much their ways of doing things meant to them, and perhaps come up with a more compassionate way of sharing and implementing my vision.

That said, however, while it would've made me a better leader, I'm not sure how much of a difference my awareness or demonstrative concern would have made in shifting their paradigm.

At the core, what was important to me then is still important to me now, and not much has changed in terms of my foundational philosophy.

I was determined to win souls for Christ, and felt strongly about the need to make sure that loyalty to time-honored practices with no root in real evangelism wasn't taking precedent over proselytizing the lost.

This was problematic for them. Too much was happening too fast. For decades, the church had been at a standstill in terms of growth, save a drifting soul here or church hopper there.

They were content with that.

I was not.

My preaching style and marketing means attracted young people by the tens, people who, let's just say, didn't come from church, and didn't look like church.

This invasive influx of outsiders made many of the leaders clutch their pearls, purses, and *persuaders* in fear. Not out of fear for their lives, but fear of losing their lifetime positions and lifelong traditions. The advent of these newcomers threatened to infringe on their rites and their rights, and they were not having it.

I don't want to spend too much time here, as the point of this anecdotal departure is only to inform you that I've led in cultures of absolute disrespect and complete reverence.

However, if you feel so inclined, you can read about my first pastorate in its entirety in my autobiography, *The Blessing Behind Closed Doors*. I detail how I overcame my challenges and how my experience there ultimately led to me starting The Word Church.

Subordinately, it's a guide for relationships, a handbook for handling grief, and a motivational tool for those struggling with issues from the past and in the present.

But even taking into consideration everything I've expressed, I am convinced there was one key difference between that leadership experience and the one I now enjoy: There is a lack of honor in our church chain of command.

It limits our growth and undermines our would-be successes. It hinders us personally and spiritually.

We afford the pastor certain influence over our agency, but this influence often stops just shy of our personal will. In other words, we'll do what he says until we disagree with what he says.

To be clear, for the most part, I believe the common approach toward the pastoral position, even in contexts consistent with how I describe my first pastorate, is one of love and admiration.

In my experience, most people who attend church on a regular basis and especially those who volunteer in ministry care deeply about their spiritual leaders, defend them rigorously if ever a person dares to speak against them, and some, so concerned with their pastor's approval, even go as far to curry favor with them.

The reason these warm feelings don't translate to the honor, deference, or esteem that run parallel with the principles of a pure theocracy has little to do with disrespectful dispositions or apathetic attitudes regarding pastoral authority.

Why then, don't lay leaders and members feel the need to always support, solve problems for, or submit to their spiritual leaders? Simply put, because we are never taught to do so.

Let's suppose it's the pastor's job to teach us to do so. How does he do it without sounding self-centered or egoistic? After all, you're pretty much telling people that they should give *you* permission to have power over *their* prerogative. And that it's their responsibility to protect and take care of you. Seriously. How does someone say that without being accused of arrogance?

Certainly, convincing someone to grant you this kind of leverage takes some oratorical finesse, lest you come off as another silver-tongued crook trying to swindle unsuspecting parishioners into giving you latitude in their lives for your predatory gain rather than their personal good. *Especially* when it comes to financial support.

If a pastor doesn't choose his words wisely, he might unintentionally trivialize the principle of pastoral privilege down to a means of feeding his ego or trying to insulate himself from fair criticism.

So, to be careful, most pastors altogether dodge the discourse that would otherwise corroborate their claims in the lives of those they've been chosen to cover. He won't broach the subject, even though there are scriptures to back him up.

But his caution is to his detriment—and his lay members'. There's a blessing in being a blessing to your pastor.

And if the pastor doesn't teach on the support he needs, financial and otherwise, then who does?

No one, thus, here we are, with well-meaning congregations across the country completely oblivious to their pastor's pressures and responsibilities.

Let me be clear.

I am not reducing the ability to effectively apprise leaders and lay members of the pastor's needs or authority to religious rhetoric, nor how well one has mastered his pitch on the matter. I think people who love their pastor and are filled with the Holy Spirit have no problem supporting, serving, and sowing into their man or woman of God.

But they can't and they won't if they don't first know or understand *the why*. Once they understand the why, *the how* follows naturally.

In cases where the how doesn't follow as a matter of course, that is, a person understands why their pastor is under pressure but doesn't know how to help, he or she will be more open and receptive to learning how.

Without question, there is another issue at hand, the one we have with authority.

If we're honest, no one really *likes* to feel like they're being lorded over. From parental issues where we sought individuation from our parents when we disliked their rules; to workplace challenges where we may feel like our boss is incompetent; to relationship issues where we may feel like or have felt like our significant other was controlling, submitting to authority tends to get a bad rap.

For black people, issues with authority may go all the way back to slavery and the African Diaspora, and while rejection of the power-over dynamic is particularly prevalent in board-driven, predominantly black churches, it isn't only in black churches.

I've spoken with white colleagues of mine who face similar challenges of rebellion or lack of respect for their position.

I've observed interactions with my white associates and their members where their members refer to them by their first name. I get the thinking behind why they permit or encourage people to address them by their first name, but I find it troubling.

In their attempt to make sure people know that they don't perceive themselves to be "anybody," they make the mistake of diluting themselves and their relationship to their members.

They may say, "Just call me, Bill."

But do you want your child to call you by your first name? Even when they become adults?

Call me crazy, but my children can never address me by my first name. I think it's dishonorable for anyone to refer to their pastor or pastor's spouse by their first name, even if the pastor says it's permissible.

I have an earned doctorate, but I prefer my members to call me, "Pastor." I'm their covering and their shepherd. Now, when I go to restaurants, hotels, and sports games, I like to use my formal title to get better service, rooms, and seats.

If a person is not a member of my church, by the way, I'm not offended in the least if they call me by my first name. I'm not their pastor.

When someone calls me something other than Pastor Vernon or Dr. Vernon, most times it's because I haven't seen them in a long time and they knew me before I was either. It's a funny thing too—what they call me reminds me of who I was when they knew me.

When I hear, "Hey, Ray!" before I recognize their face, I know they had to grow up with me.

When I hear, "Little Rainnell," I know it's a family member.

And I'm fine with both those scenarios, but at church, I'm Pastor Vernon.

Your first lady or first man, even if you're old enough to be their parent, is not your son or daughter. We refer to my wife as, "Lady Vernon" at church. Perhaps you can find a similar way of addressing your pastor's spouse.

At the end of the day, it is the pastor's responsibility to create a culture of honor and respect, but if he doesn't, it doesn't absolve you of your obligation to honor and respect him. If in reading this, you realize that you or members of your church haven't been treating your pastor and first lady this way, be the catalyst.

Start a movement that says, "In our church, we hold our man and woman in the highest regard and will treat them with the honor they deserve."

In *The 360 Degree Leader: Developing Your Influence from Anywhere in the Organization*, John Maxwell speaks explicitly to this: "Leadership is more disposition than position—influence others from wherever you are."[2]

It doesn't matter whether you are paid staff or unpaid staff, a deacon or an usher, you can help set the tone.

Now, if you're in a church where your pastor has committed an immoral act, there is an ongoing issue with lack of transparency, or some other integrity issue that has stained his character in such a way that you cannot respect him, rather than dishonor him, move on.

What people don't realize is that it is not authority in and of itself that people take issue with, it is the *abuse of authority*, or the fear that surrendering to another's authority means you give up your personal power in a way that diminishes your sense of self-worth.

What I am attempting to do in this book is explain why honoring, supporting, and serving your pastor is important. These are all mutually inclusive events by the way—each one is dependent on the other. There can be no honor where there is no support, there can be no support where there is no service, and there can be no service where there is no honor.

Most times when we think about honor, we think about submission, and while that's true, honor is about more than submission, and so is this book. As a matter-of-fact, submission represents only a fraction of what I want you to glean from this.

To honor is to value, to revere, to hold in high esteem. When we honor our pastors, we value them as truthtellers who impart the ultimate Truth into our lives. Truth that we and the world need desperately.

We revere them as God's own, His shepherds, who lead and guide us in the ways of Christ.

We recognize the significance of their position and the gravity of their burdens as best we can, and we incline ourselves in service of them however we can.

But rather than simply admonish or lecture you on why you should do this, I want to help you understand your pastor's predicament and (we've finally made it to the circumference of our text) their pressures.

Regardless of the size of your church, your pastor is under some kind of pressure.

You may say, "But we only have fifty members." Then he's under pressure to grow.

"We have five-hundred members." Then he's under pressure to maintain.

"We have thousands of people." He's under pressure to provide more room.

In my second work, *Size Does Matter: Moving Your Ministry From Micro to Mega*, I canvass the different stages of growth and talk about things you can do at every level. I cover the three pressures I just mentioned at length, offering strategies for how to tackle each one.

Because there are levels to this. Whether you're at a mega or startup ministry, your pastor is under more pressure than you know.

In this book, I aim first to accentuate the pressures you're already familiar with, giving you an eye-witness account of the stresses of pastoring; and second, to acquaint you with the ones that may be foreign to you.

I believe that if you have a better sense of what it is to be in your pastor's shoes, you'll think about and act differently toward him. The point is not to get you to feel sympathy for him, but to get you to understand his plight.

It is my hope that by the end of this book, you'll feel a deeper respect and appreciation for the inevitable pressures your pastor feels daily.

---

[1] (Wallace, et al., 2011)

[2] (Maxwell, 2011 p. 56)

THEOLOGICAL BASIS

II Corinthians 11:28 (NASB) says, "Apart from such external things, there is the daily pressure on me of concern for all the churches."

In case you were wondering, this scripture is where the inspiration for this book came from.

In context, we know that the Apostle Paul, the talented tentmaker from Tarsus, has in the previous scriptures listed a litany of losses he's experienced, chronicling the arduous undertakings he'd been through.

He talks about how he had been beaten, abandoned, famished, and persecuted. He describes all he's had to bear, including opposition and contempt from his haters, in the name of establishing the Judeo-Christian Church.

And yet, this persecution appears to have been less bothersome than the burden he felt for the churches he covered.

Notice the distinction Paul makes between all that he's endured and the "daily pressure" he faces. He calls the former "external"—these were things that affected his body. The distinction here is important because it implies that his "concern for all the churches" affected him in a much deeper sense; it was internal, emotional, psychological.

And as it was with Paul, it is with your pastor. Pastoring is all-encompassing work. While much of what we do is external—preaching, teaching, visiting, marrying, burying, meeting; the prerequisite to everything we do is internal, thinking, meditating, sensing, determining, discovering, learning, questioning, praying, realizing, calculating.

Many of these processes, both internal and external, are happening simultaneously, and they all consume our energy. But the internal processes are decidedly more exhausting.

What follows in this quick read is everything your pastor wants you to know, but didn't know how to tell you.

ONE | **WHO IS YOUR PASTOR?**

To care about your pastor's pressures, you should first determine who your pastor is. I know that sounds simplistic, but you'd be amazed at how many people go from church to church with no devotion to any one pastor.

Or, they might visit a church weekly because they like the pastor's preaching, but haven't taken the next step in terms of commitment. They attend, but they're not really connected.

You must decide who your pastor is.

I often tell other pastors eager to tell me about the size of their ministry, "Don't tell me who you're over, until you tell me who you're under."

I'm not asking you to follow advice that I don't personally adhere to.

My pastor is Bishop Joey Johnson. From the time he came into my life some eighteen years ago, he's never left me and I've never left him.

I believe I surpassed him in church attendance in my third year, and some of my colleagues were quick to point out that while Bishop was a good place to start, I probably needed someone who could better relate to the challenges I faced in terms of growth.

I understood where they were coming from, but I didn't and I don't agree with that rationale. Whenever a peer makes this suggestion, I simply and succinctly reply, "Just because your behind gets bigger than your mama's behind, she's still your mama."

I feel the same honor and respect for Bishop Joey now as I did when The Word Church was nothing more than an idea in my mind. As a matter of fact, when I think about it, I honor and respect him even more than I did back then.

I have long settled in my mind and spirit that I'm with Joey Johnson and that isn't going to change because of the size of my church.

Now, I do have "uncles" and "brothers" in the ministry as I like to call them, who I can swap stories with about ministry, but I have but one spiritual father and I'm unapologetically loyal and submitted to him.

If Lady Vernon has an issue that she needs to discuss with someone other than me, she knows she can call Bishop Joey, without telling me beforehand.

I make very few major decisions without first seeking his advice. If he disagrees with a decision I'm about to make, I think long and hard about whether it's worth it for me to make that decision. The few times I have strayed from his wise counsel, I later lamented my choice to do so.

If I do something stupid in ministry that requires me to sit down for a season, Bishop Joey is in charge and I'll return only when he deems it appropriate. If he decides that I am not to return, he'll decide who the next pastor is. If I die, Bishop Joey and Lady Vernon are in charge and they'll execute the plan we have in place for that scenario.

So, who is *your* pastor? You can't have two pastors like you can't have two spouses. You need one voice of God on earth. Just one. Sure, you can listen to the messages of other pastors, and in a moment, we'll review a scripture where Paul speaks to this directly,

But in terms of where you go to get fed spiritually, there should be a real relationship with your pastor that supersedes any other pastor's word in your life.

If you continually listen to more than one pastor, at some point, their ideas or interpretations may conflict, and you'll be forced to choose. Avoid this conundrum by establishing who your pastor is.

Once you do, take your relationship with him as serious as you do the most important relationships in your life.

My suggested hierarchy goes like this: spouse, children, close family, then pastor. He's responsible for speaking to you directly from God every week. Besides the relationships I just mentioned, what others could possibly come before the one you have with him?

If your pastor is the person you would call if your wife left you, the person you would expect at your side if your baby was diagnosed with cancer, the person you would want to lay hands on you if you were about to lose your mind, he is indispensable to you, and you should treat him as such.

In one of his letters to the Corinthians, Paul reinforces the idea of one pastor.

He says in I Corinthians 4:14-16 (NLT), "¹⁴I am not writing these things to shame you, but to warn you as my beloved children. ¹⁵For even if you had ten thousand others to teach you about Christ, you have only one spiritual father. For I became your father in Christ Jesus when I preached the Good News to you. ¹⁶So I urge you to imitate me."

What kind of narcissistic trip is Paul on, anyway? Imitate *him*? Not *Jesus*?! (*gasp!*)

Okay, so, no. Paul is not being arrogant or narcissistic here. In the words of Dr. Mack King Carter, we dare not "attack this text with some narrow, provincial, cognitive appropriation." In simpler terms, let's not be that petty in our thinking.

Paul is saying, "Follow me, as I follow Christ. I'm here with you, in the flesh, Jesus is not."

I echo Paul's sentiment. If one of my leaders said to me, "Pastor, I'm following Jesus," my response would be, "No you're not, because He's not here."

Yes, He's in our hearts and with us in Spirit. But stay with me.

God places pastors in our lives to lead us in the local church, using His model. Your pastor is who you follow.

As such, oftentimes, you'll hear pastors say, "my members," when referring to those who have joined their church, in the same way that parents say, "these are my children," when referring to their sons and daughters.

When you introduce your kids to someone they've never met, you don't say, "These are God's children, Jane and John."

No, you say that these are "my children," because they are. Even if you didn't birth them, say, in the case of a blended family, you still refer to them as "my children" when you're the one taking care of them.

Psalms 24:1 (NLT) says, "The earth is the Lord's, and everything in it. The world and all its people belong to him," so we know for certain that we're all God's property.

Pastors and Christian parents alike know that sovereignly and ultimately, church members are God's members and our children are His children, yet the common usage is to identify them as our own.

There's something else we should observe in Paul's language here. He calls himself their "father." This lends credence to the idea that Paul counts his responsibility as an authoritative figure with considerable weight. It's the same duty a parent feels for their child. What a powerful paragon of a pastor's relationship with his members.

Later, Paul says in I Corinthians 9:1-2, "¹Am I not free? Am I not an apostle? Have I not seen Jesus our Lord? Are you not **my work** in the Lord? ²If to others I am not an apostle, at least I am to you; for you are the seal of my apostleship in the Lord. (*emphasis mine*)

Paul's questions here are rhetorical in nature, but for good reason. When he asks, "Am I not an apostle?" and "Have I not seen Jesus our Lord?" he is self-affirming his position as one sent by God. He says in effect, "I'm your pastor. You better recognize."

Then he probes them further. "Are you not my work?"

Notice he didn't say or ask if they were Jesus' work. He assumes a possessive, protective, paternal role because he is the one laboring among them and on their behalf *in the name of the Lord*.

So, like Paul, when pastors refer to church members this way, as their "work," it is from a spiritual perspective, particularly when referencing those who have been with him or her for a long time. This type of attachment to our members is one of affection, and it stems from protection, not possession; from intimacy, not intimidation.

Lest I be labeled a heretic let's be crystal clear: You never praise or worship anybody but Jesus. Your pastor is not God; he is not Jesus. He is the voice of God, but he is not God and be careful not to regard him as such. He's not perfect and he won't ever be. Your pastor is human and capable of failing you.

He has faults just like you do. Yes, he's accepted a higher calling that positions him above you in terms of spiritual leadership, but he is not God. God is God. Remember that, always. Put Him first, and have complete and total faith in Him and Him only.

Now, back to the point.

I love the way Paul frames his relationship with the church at Corinth and if you read closely, you'll gain a better understanding of why his view is applicable to us even today, thousands of years later.

If you've been with your pastor for a long time, it's likely that you have his spiritual DNA. While you have your own unique gifts and abilities, you've taken on some of his. He baptized, discipled, taught, mentored, and trained you. You're his work. He counseled and married you. In terms of a spiritual covering, he's all you know.

If you were to betray your pastor in some way today, yes, it would change the nature of your relationship, but it wouldn't change the fact that you share his spiritual DNA, and you couldn't change it if you wanted to, no more than you could change being related to your mother or father just because they upset you.

Long after you've moved on, your pastor's influence remains with you. Therefore, it's highly important that you choose your pastor wisely and that you don't minimize your relationship with him because at both conscious and subconscious levels, his thinking, attitudes, teaching, and behaviors will shape you.

I want to use this notion as a segue to a common complaint I hear from people who leave the church.

"My pastor hurt me," they say.

Well, so did your man, but you didn't leave him. Your wife is always dogging you, but you're still with her. Your boss doesn't respect you in the least, and still, you work for him.

But the pastor says one wrong thing, and you're too hurt to go on? You can't bear to attend the church anymore? *Really?* Why is it so easy for us to walk away from church when we're wounded, but we don't walk away when friends, bosses, or close family members wound us?

It's impossible to be in relationship with someone and never see their bad side. Those who work in proximity to me know that because of how close they are, when they're in my personal quarters, sometimes, the bullets will fly.

I'll never abuse my authority—I fear God too much to disrespect his people or exploit my call. But if I have a moment, my staff must be mature enough to absorb the blow and keep it moving.

The point is, love your pastor, even when you see the worst of him. He needs to know that he can trust you to still have his back, even if he loses it one day and says something he shouldn't have said.

Your relationship with your pastor shouldn't feel oppressive, however. If your pastor is always angry, constantly cursing somebody out, and emasculating his leaders, something else is going on and no person should stay in a verbally, emotionally, or spiritually abusive relationship.

I trust that is not the case and I want you to try to explain why he may at times speak in a way that belies his good intentions.

On weekends, your pastor hears all kinds of stories. A wife stepped out on her husband, a mother finds out her child is being molested by a family friend, a man finds out he's been diagnosed with a life-threatening disease, a woman discovers porn on her son's cell phone, a husband beat his wife the night before.

On top of hearing all this, your pastor is dealing with the fact that his wife just lost her job so they're down to one income, the kids did something stupid that morning on the way to church, and he just found out that a bill that was supposed to be paid months ago never got paid and now there's a bigger issue. Plus, he didn't get much sleep the night before, so he already wasn't in the best of moods.

Now, he's preached forty-five minutes, and one after another, for another twenty minutes, people are telling him story after story like the ones I just mentioned. And he's listening, and praying, and touching…

Remember when the woman touched the hem of Jesus' garment? He recognized the pull immediately. He felt the power leave him.

Imagine the pull of hearing situations like these back-to-back, again, after you expended all your energy preaching? That's what your pastor experiences every weekend.

Lady Vernon and I do it five times every weekend, and when we get home on Sunday evening, we sit in the shower, worn out, completely spent. Sometimes, we're being summoned for dinner, but we're too tired to move.

A psychologist who attends our church asked me one day, "What do you guys do to rinse?"

"Rinse?" I asked.

"Yes. You take in so much toxicity. You have to purge. Take good vacations, get good massages, take adequate mental breaks. Make sure you rinse."

Lady Vernon and I are blessed to be in a situation where we can rinse, and rinse regularly. We have competent staff, good systems in place, and the resources to take our breaks when we need them.

It wasn't always this way, however. And when it wasn't, it showed in my leadership and in my relationships.

Patience has never been my strongest quality, though today, I am much more thoughtful and less reactive in situations that test it than I was in my early days of pastoring The Word Church.

But back then, being under immense pressure, hearing all the heartrending accounts of people's daily struggles, combined with lack of resting and rinsing, I'm sure there are times my staff got the worst of me.

I make this point for two reasons.

One, to share what pastors are dealing with at any given point in time so that you understand why, under this kind of duress, they may say the wrong thing; and two, so that you recognize why they need your support and loyalty when they have these moments.

My spiritual daughter, Jennifer, who's been with me since she was five, put it this way in her book, *Who's Running Your Church?*

> A marginless standard of living of and its related pressures is damaging to our relationships. If you're a pastor, your members need you. If you're staff, your pastor needs you. If you're an administrator, your team needs you. But if you're...wrecked, nobody needs you—that is until you've given your mind the rest it deserves.[3]

We'll cover this more later, but the point she was making is that when you constantly operate on the margins because you don't get a chance to rest, you'll act out and burn out, and the mind will eventually shut down for rest anyway. At that point, you're "wrecked."

Now that you realize what we're up against on the weekends (that is to say nothing of the rest of the week), I hope you'll be mindful of the importance of getting your pastor to a place where he can avoid getting wrecked, and getting him to a place where he can rest and rinse too.

---

3 (Wainwright, et al., 2014 p. 331)

TWO | **THE PRESSURE TO PLAN**

Planning is a rigorous discipline, and as with any discipline, it requires considerable time, consistent effort, and concerted application.

It is ultimately your pastor's responsibility to plan everything the church is going to do. If he's fortunate, he has staff to support him and help him implement his ideas. But whether he has a team to help him execute his goals or not, the buck starts and stops with him.

For a pastor, planning is a complex practice, and one move often involves making multiple decisions. For example, should he add a service? change locations? invest in rebranding? hire additional staff? let some staff go?

With each of these decisions comes a multitude of mini decisions, each of which will directly affect how others perceive his leadership, including you.

If he makes a move and then fails, his competence will be questioned. If he makes a move and succeeds, higher expectations for his future moves will follow. If he doesn't make moves at all, people will say he lacks vision or decisiveness.

See the problem here? Or should I say, the *pressure?*

A great part of his responsibility is to be the visionary. He has to have the emotional objectivity and spiritual sensitivity to analyze where the church is at any given point in time, and then with that in mind, come up with actionable ideas about where he wants to lead next. Then, he must develop a strategy for getting to said destination.

To be clear, these can't be mere pie-in-the-sky ideas—otherwise, he's not a visionary, he's a dreamer. He must conceptualize and then concretize ways to get the church to the next level.

For pastors who are not content with the size of their ministry, this pressure may be particularly taxing. Atop everything else, the desire to grow a ministry comes tethered to many a sleepless night.

He doesn't want to downplay the call to evangelize the lost by following the latest fads or compromise the sacredness of soul-saving work by watering down the Word of

God with cheap marketing tactics, yet, he must constantly think of new ways to attract newcomers.

Planning requires creativity and regimented practices. He has to think about the church calendar, things that will bring excitement to the ministry, his preaching schedule, and community events the church should be involved in.

He must plan every detail of the weekend, taking nothing for granted, from what he's going to wear to the worship selections. If there are screens, the backgrounds must be chosen to complement his wardrobe. Everything should be planned. No one should be winging it on Sunday morning, least of all, him. And he can't do all the planning for the weekend the week of or the week before. Some things need to be planned out well in advance, so he has to be strategic in rationing out specific time just for this.

I tell all the pastors whom I cover to take a calendar, and all the ideas they've been ruminating over, and go away for at least two to three weeks out of the year to plan for the upcoming year.

Imagine the pressure of planning for a year that has not arrived yet, having no idea what that year will bring. Meanwhile, you still have to prepare for and deal with the challenges and events of the current year.

It's true that we should all be conscious of our future. But your pastor is planning for his personal future *and* the future of the ministry.

And when it comes to the future of the ministry, his plan almost has to be prophetic. He has to have a feel for where God is moving and what He wants to do next, and therein lies another pressure, the pressure to pray.

You might say that prayer shouldn't be a pressure, that it's every Christian's duty, and you'd be right. About the last part, anyway. But there is a pressure to pray, because whereas some people may "get away" with not praying and be unaware of a real difference in their daily occupation, for a pastor, the absence of prayer in our lives is painfully evident in our vocational pursuits.

"A minister may fill his pews, his communion roll, the mouths of the public, but what that minister is on his knees in secret before God Almighty, that he is and no more."[4]

It doesn't matter how many people attended on a Sunday, how much money we brought in, or even how well our sermon went over...if we lack a genuine prayer life.

Seventeenth-century theologian John Owens said it this way:

> What the Church needs to-day is not more ma-
> chinery or better, not new organizations or more
> and novel methods, but men whom the Holy Ghost
> can use—men of prayer, men mighty in prayer. The
> Holy Ghost does not flow through methods, but
> through men. He does not come on machinery, but
> on men. He does not anoint plans, but men—men
> of prayer.[5]

Praying, especially when in search of direction, requires perseverance and close fellowship with God. You certainly don't want to make a move without seeking God's face, thus, praying and planning go hand-in-hand.

I watched a movie some time ago called, *Margin Call*. Without giving the entire movie away, there is one scene I want to share with you.

A CEO is sitting at a table with his staff late into the night. An emergency meeting is underway because a young analyst on the team has discovered that the company is on the brink of a major financial crisis.

The CEO asks the analyst to explain to him exactly what's happening.

He (the CEO) says, "And please, speak as you might to a young child," which was funny to me, because I often say this to my staff when asking them to explain a complex or detailed problem. But he takes it one step further.

"Or a golden retriever. It wasn't brains that got me here. I can assure you of that."

Anyway, the analyst explains the issue. The CEO, who makes eight figures, quickly realizing the gravity of the situation thinks for a minute and then says, "Do you care to know why I earn the big bucks?"

The analyst answers, "Yes."

"I'm here for one reason and one reason alone...to guess what the music might do a week, a month, a year from now. That's it. Nothing more. And standing here tonight, I'm afraid that I don't hear a thing. Just silence."

As a pastor, the feeling he describes is not unlike the pressure we as pastors feel to sense the next move of God, and, to use his analogy, once we do hear the music, how do we inspire our congregations to get in step with the melody? Especially if the idea is a radical one?

As the leaders of our organizations, we must make big decisions—decisions for which we get the credit if all goes well, and all the blame if it ends up being an epic failure. While we need our team to help us sort through details and implement our ideas, we get paid to see, to hear, to sense, to feel.

When he's praying about and planning his preaching schedule there are pragmatic considerations to factor in.

For example, at The Word Church, the first quarter seems to be our highest giving season. Therefore, I typically plan to preach about tithing and giving during this time. But if we're in a particularly bad economy where people are losing jobs left and right, then it's important that I think about how that's going to play out in the lives of my members, and remember to adjust my teaching accordingly.

Making this adjustment also bespeaks the pressure to be prophetic, which can be tricky when you're already planned out.

When I say 'prophetic,' I'm referring to the social justice issues of our day and being sensitive to how court decisions, government policies, law enforcement misconduct, and crime and job rates affect those who I cover.

If something happens that rocks our city—an unarmed child gets killed by a police officer or a family gets burned out of their home—I have to modify my message to meet the emotional needs of my members.

But sometimes, I need to adjust my message when something good happens. When the Cavs won the 2016 NBA world championship, it was, by all accounts, a historic moment for our city. Clevelanders were ecstatic and morale in the city was electric. Every local (and some national) news story headline was some iteration of, "The Curse is Over," so that's exactly what I preached. After a fifty-two-year sports championship drought, how could I not adapt my message and tie our city's triumph to my members' personal trials?

But it's not just the preaching. He has to plan his breaks, keeping his personal obligations in mind, so that he doesn't accept a date to perform a wedding ceremony on the same day his son is graduating from college.

And there's that pesky pressure even when she takes a vacation, presumably to get *away* from pressure. When he's not there, people don't give as much. No matter how many massages he gets to relax his mind, he can never escape the knowledge that his presence at church, or lack thereof, affects the offering.

It's important to note that in the midst of all our plans, God has His own. He has a plan for every pastor whom He has called to lead and shepherd His people. And "the truth is, the plans God has for you are always bigger than you are, and they are never going to be something you can pull off easily and in your own strength."[6]

But that reality doesn't release us from our responsibility to plan, it reinforces it. Passive or poor planning on our part, coupled with a pathetic prayer life, can and will adversely affect what God plans to do.

I agree with John Maxwell, who says that everything rises and falls on leadership. And while most of us understand that God ultimately determines our ministry's growth or effectiveness, I believe that if we're not mindful, we can hinder, delay, or altogether prevent our progress.

---

[4] (Keller, 2014)

[5] (Bounds, 2012)

[6] (Houston, 2015)

THREE | **THE PRESSURE TO PREACH**

Every week, usually twice a week, pastors must come up with something to say that doesn't put folk to sleep. They have to tell the same old stories, in fresh, new ways.

He's covered just about every relevant topic he can think of. He's done every miracle twice, he's preached on the Fruit of the Spirit, the Gifts of the Spirit, prayer, faith, love, marriage, kids, forgiveness, and money.

No matter how many times he preaches on Daniel and the Lion's Den, he still comes out alive in the end, Moses' bush is still burning, and after learning his lesson, The Prodigal Son remains back home chilling at the crib, with his brother still sulking and side-eyeing him.

His Boss has told him that he only gets one book to teach out of, and while it's comprised of sixty-six individual books, some of those aren't really fair game for prime-time Sunday morning. Let's be honest. Have you ever been eager to hear about a message on Leviticus?

Now, as a pastor, I have to know the book of Zephaniah, but I don't see many people shouting on a sermon from it.

I say often, the entire Bible is true, but the entire Bible is not exciting. It's not meant to be.

But because it isn't, we're limited to the books with Bathsheba-gate like scandals, Abraham-and-Isaac-going-up-the-mountain-like suspense, and of course the Gospels, which contain the heartening happy endings from which we derive our holiday homilies. There are other books with liberating promises and transformative principles that work well on weekends too—still...we don't get the *whole* Bible.

When we do cover some of the tough stories of the Old Testament—and they are relevant because they did happen—we are confronted with the question: How do we build a bridge to contemporize old covenant principles with new covenant truths?

Your pastor has taught all the great stories of the Old Testament and New. He's preached the same things so often that he's now calling his second versions, "The Remix."

He's had TVs, beds, cars, and animals on the stage. In fact, he's used so many illustrations that he feels like he's running out of ideas and the weekend seems to come so fast, he often feels that he doesn't have time to step away long enough to come up with original ones.

In *The Creative Leader*, Ed Young makes the case for why it's important to switch up your approach so that your listeners don't get bored. He says, "If you're going to keep your audience guessing [*read: intrigued*], if you're going to keep the connectivity high, you've got to keep the predictability low."[7]

So, your pastor has tried to retool his routine a few times so as not to become predictable, but now he fears he might be becoming predictably unpredictable, which only adds to the pressure, because he knows that people expect him to come up with new ways of engaging them.

Some people have been at the church for a decade or longer, and still look for their pastor to say something they have never heard before.

For those pastors who aren't seminary trained, there's another layer of difficulty to their preparation because they have to work through hermeneutic processes without the benefit of the scholarship that comes from doing concentrated theological coursework. Without some form of doctrinal education, they risk straying away from the text, which is the last thing any self-respecting pastor wants to do. This in turn limits what they can preach.

Rather than gamble with misinterpretations of the Word, they'll cling to what they know—biblical blankies, I like to call them. After all, he's less likely to suffer a biblical blunder, when he sticks to scriptural passages that are familiar and comfortable.

But of course, the consequence of this is what we've already addressed—repetitive, *remixed*, preaching.

I'm a trained seminarian, and encourage every pastor to make theological education a priority. Not only does it give your preaching depth, the level of understanding you'll gain from studying the Bible (and other religions) from an academic standpoint, it will give you a newfound respect for what you already love, deepen your faith, and preclude you—for the most part—from straining texts.

But then there's the various forms of criticism that you must engage in your preparation: source, redaction, narrative, literary, textual, and exegetical, to name a few, where you are essentially arguing with the text, distilling from it what no longer applies, bearing in mind cultural nuances, and carefully noting the linguistic differences from today's language based on Greek or Hebrew etymology.

In doing all this, you must be careful to prep your message in such a way that it is easily grasped by everyone listening to you, chiefly to the lost souls in search of a savior. To that end "...language matters, and should not be used to obscure our view of God but rather bring it in to sharper focus."[8]

It is hard work. What you listen to for forty minutes took nine hours (or more) to prepare. Double that if there is a midweek Bible Study. If he teaches other classes through-out the week, keep piling the hours on.

By default, the rigors of academia require a higher form of discipline in your studies than personal study alone. This makes you a lot more circumspect in your preaching and teaching and while your style, philosophy, and ap-proach may evolve over time, the method stays with you.

Every bit of this pressure gets compounded if—God for-bid—he happens to be bi-vocational. Trust me, it's not even the will of God to try to work eight hours and pastor.

Bi-vocationalism leads to life characterized by busyness and burnout. In busyness and burnout there is no calm and silence, only the cacophony of distraction and depression.

Without calm and silence, it's difficult to hear God's heart, thus, we have to "keep...from being so busy that [we] can no longer hear the voice of God who speaks in silence."[9]

If your pastor is in a position that requires him to both lead the church and work eight hours at another job, one of your main goals as a part of his supporting cast is to team up with other church staff and figure out a way to get him off that job.

Pastoring, at any level, is full-time work.

Conceivably, pastors with more members and more staff may have more responsibility, but a pastor with a small church may face more pressure because the church is small.

He has to determine why the church isn't growing and figure out better ways of attracting the lost or securing the back door so that people aren't coming in the front door, having an emotional experience, and then exiting through the rear to never return.

He needs time to think about how to disciple the members he has. He needs energy to pour back into those who need him the most. He needs something left in the tank so he can be creative and sharpen his skills.

I've said on occasion that we only get one energy tank a day. We don't get separate tanks for our job, our spouse, our kids, and whatever else we've decided is important to us. Because we only get one tank, it's critical for us to manage our energy efficiently, because once it's gone, it's gone.

Consider your pastor's tank. If his first job requires one-third of his day, it's probable that his first job is also consuming the biggest chunk of his energy.

Now, he has to try to muster up whatever energy he has left to connect with his wife, spend time with his kids, and work on church stuff? And not just the stuff—what about his time in and with the actual Word of God? The time he needs to cultivate his own closeness with the Creator so he can be in sync with where He is and what He wants him to do? The time he needs to study, meditate, and ruminate on what he's reading to prepare a worthy message? Consider this:

> How can...sermons be worth listening to, if we our-selves [pastors] have not had the time to eat and digest the Word? Because this is what preaching is: digesting the Word so that instead of just a set of notes, we carry something internal—a kind of pregnancy.[10]

To "eat and digest the Word" is to investigate it. It is to interact with it; to immerse yourself so deeply in its trea-sures that it feels intimate. Every person who is or has ever been in a serious relationship knows (or rather they should) that intimacy is an investment; a cognitive, calcu-lated investment of which the intent is to foster emotional connectedness and bring you closer to the one you've cho-sen to invest in. This kind of investment is a prerequisite for solid, sincere, God-breathed preaching.

One can hardly do that if he's overwhelmed with other responsibilities that gnaw away at the time he would devote to his vocational work otherwise.

Some people or some things in the *job-family-home-sermon prep/church* equation are going to get short-changed and we all know it's not going to be the job, because that's primarily how he feeds himself and his family.

He may be able to get a pass a few nights a week from his wife because she supports him and will hold down the house as much as she can to give him the time he needs for his other obligations, but this kind of one-sided relational responsibility distribution will only last but so long before it starts to breed other problems.

By process of elimination, we know what's going to end up getting the short end of the stick...

To be fair, most bi-vocational pastors I know are doing the best they can to do it all, so this isn't an indictment on their effort as much as it is an appraisal of their effectiveness in their efforts.

If he has to keep up this kind of pace for any appreciable amount of time, he's going to eventually suffer burnout, and the last thing you want is a burnt-out pastor.

Once burnout begins, half-hearted hermeneutics and platitudinous preaching replace rhetorically polished reasoning. He's probably short-tempered too, "in one of those moods," as my staff used to describe me, when I'd cavil about everything because everything irritated me.

At this point, he's functioning on fumes, and he is incapable of doing his best work at work, at home, or at church.

If he completely exhausts his energy reserves because he can't take or catch a break, he may seek escape in some form of unhealthy behavior. The decision to engage in unhealthy behaviors isn't usually a conscious one—he's way too overwhelmed to be mindful. It is a decision made at a subconscious level to manage his stress, a coping mechanism. It happens subtly. His guards are down. He's not on his face because he feels he can't afford to put his head down. There's too much going on.

So now, he's not only under pressure, he's under siege. The enemy is coming for him in whatever way he can, because he's vulnerable, and Satan knows it.

I'm sure by now, you see the problem here.

You want your pastor rested and refreshed, with margin in his life so that he has room to work a little more when he needs to without jeopardizing his emotional and spiritual health. Sure, there'll be seasons when he's going to have to put in more hours than normal. But this should be the exception and not the rule.

You want him at his best, with his boundaries intact so that he can preserve the time he needs for reflection, planning, and preparation; so that he can be both steward and student, engaging his Word with his head and heart.

E. M. Bounds places the heart above all else in terms of preparation. "A prepared heart is much better than a prepared sermon. A prepared heart will make a prepared sermon."[11]

To give you some personal perspective, I spend eight to ten hours on one message. I've read about pastors that spend ten to twenty hours preparing a message. And some who spend only one or two.

An article by Eddie McKiddie on pastoralized.com mentions the following other well-known pastors and how much time they take to prepare:

Mark Driscoll | 1 to 2 Hours

A few years back, Pastor Driscoll tweeted, "Prepping 2 sermons today. Thankfully, a sermon takes about as long to prep as preach."

This tweet inspired incredulity and curiosity alike from many pastors, prompting him to conduct a Q & A session on Facebook. Here is an excerpt from that conversation explaining how he does it:

By God's grace my memory is very unusual. I can still remember a section of a book I read 20 years ago while preaching and roll with it. I've also never sat down to memorize a Bible verse. Yet, many just stick, and I can pull them up from memory as I go. Lastly, I'm a verbal processor. I think out loud, which is what preaching is for me. A degree in speech and over 10,000 hours of preaching experience also helps. And most importantly and thankfully, the Holy Spirit always helps.

When I get up to preach, the jokes, illustrations, cross-references, and closing happen extemporaneously. I never teach others how to preach, as my method is not exactly a replicable method—nor a suggested one. But it works for me.

Tim Keller *(Small Rural Church)* | 6 to 8 hours

Tim Keller *(Big Manhattan Church)* | 14 to 16 hours

John Piper | All day Friday, half-day Saturday

Matt Chandler | All day Tuesday, all day Thursday

Kent Hughes | 20 hours

John MacArthur | 32 hours [12]

Pastor Tim Keller had an interesting approach. You may have noticed he spends more hours preparing for his message at the bigger church. This is what he said about the smaller one:

> I would not advise younger ministers to spend so much time [on sermon preparation], however. The main way to become a good preacher is to preach a lot, and to spend tons of time in people work–that is how you grow from becoming not just a Bible commentator but a flesh and blood preacher. When I was a pastor without a large staff I put in 6-8 hours on a sermon.[13]

(For an explanation of the prep method of each pastor listed here, check the notes and read the article in full.)

The variance in the number of hours a pastor needs to prepare could be due to a number of things—how quickly he can "get in the zone," whether his study time is uninterrupted and free from distractions, his experience, whether the sermon is a revised version of a previous sermon—all these things will all affect the amount of time it takes him to get through the groundwork of his message.

One other note you may find interesting about the pressure your pastor feels when preparing his sermon, some of which I alluded to earlier in the chapter:

> ...Sometimes, a sermon can come to us in one hour. Other weeks we are fighting for each sen-

tence. But always, whether it takes an hour or eight hours, we are looking for the fresh angle, a way of saying it, that is not necessarily original—it doesn't need to be original—but does justice to the originality of the text...[But] people don't see this work. It can't be accounted for.[14]

Even if you don't see it, however, this work is very much still taking place. And if it isn't, eventually, it will show. Talent and charisma can be wonderful complements to the anointing, but they cannot replace it.

It's been said that preaching a one-hour sermon is the equivalent of working a forty-hour workweek. Preaching is indeed, one of the most arduous tasks in the world.

A quick Google search will reveal that this comparison is widely disputed, with some pastors even posting articles to the contrary, saying that they'd never compare a sixty-minute sermon to working forty hours.

While I can't speak to their experience or previous work, I can speak to my own.

Prior to pastoring, I worked construction twelve hours a day. It is strenuous, exhausting labor. While the laboriousness of preaching may lend itself to conflicting views, I think it's safe to say that no one would argue the physical demand of carrying twenty-eight to thirty pound cinderblocks.

In addition to blocks, I also lifted and carried drywall. Do you see where I'm going with this? *No?* Okay. Well, let me say it plainly.

I was markedly more rested doing that than I am now preaching multiple services on weekends.

Back then, I would leave work and go play basketball. Now, after I get through speaking, touching, and hugging, I'm beat. Preaching completely enervates my energy. I have nothing left. Sometimes, I'm too tired to sleep.

Have you ever been so tired you couldn't fall asleep? It's a feeling that is difficult to define in a way that those who are not practitioners of the task will understand, but I hope my description helps.

Even if your pastor only does one service, I'm sure that once the weekend is over, he too is fatigued. The burden that befalls him is more than just the preaching itself; it's the spiritual pull. It's the virtue coming out of him. It's the Holy Spirit moving.

It's the weight of wondering if the message he preached ministered to those who needed it most.

It's the awareness that God is judging, people are listening, and your family and staff are depending on you. Souls are at stake. The livelihoods of those you employ hang on whether you consistently hit the ball over the fence. Sure, they could get another job, but at this point, they earn their pay by working for you.

As a pastor, you give everything you have, specifically, but not exclusively, when you preach.

It is an intense, internal, all-encompassing vortex of your mental, spiritual, emotional, and physiological energy; an arresting experience exacerbated by its expedience.

Now envision—with all this in mind—what it must be like for him every time he grabs the mic to minister. And if he must minister at multiple services, multiply this effect by however many services there are.

Personally, I preach four times every weekend (once on Saturday, three on Sunday), and three times on Wednesdays, and I'm telling you, my staff and family know, Monday and Thursday are my recovery days.

Your pastor's rhythm of renewal is something else to be mindful of. Unless he's instructed you otherwise, try to refrain from reaching out to him on the days following heavy ministry days. If he calls you to check in, fine, give him the updates he needs, but if he doesn't, give him a day (or at least the morning), to recoup his energy.

---

[7] (Young, 2006 p. 114)

[8] (Stackhouse, et al., 2014 p. 152)

[9] (Nouwen, 2016 p. 67)

[10] (Stackhouse, et al., 2014 p. 137)

[11] (Bounds, 2012)

[12] (McKiddie, 2013)

[13] Ibid

[14] (Stackhouse, et al., 2014 p. 137)

FOUR | **THE PRESSURE TO PERFORM**

Your pastor is an actor.

You didn't know? Then, he's probably very good.

He may not be a thespian of the usual sort, but he is indeed a performer. Let me explain.

Your pastor has days he wishes he did not have to go to work, just like you. There are times when he and the first lady are en route to Sunday morning service, and they're irritated. With one another.

You didn't know that either?

Yes, your pastor and first lady sometimes fall out, just like you and your spouse. And of course, it happens at the worst possible time.

They're in the car in the middle of "heated fellowship" seconds before they arrive at the church. As much as they want to stay in the car and hash it out, duty calls, and they must respond.

So, they fling open their doors and quickly transform their expressions from frowns and frustration to bright and breezy.

"Hey, Baby! How are you? Wow, look at how adorable she is!" She says, arms outstretched to the beaming mother coming over to speak to her with a baby on her hip.

"Deacon, James! So good to see you this morning!" He says with an obligatory grin to the brother coming over for a quick embrace.

They continue to greet every person, hugging and smiling...but still seething on the inside. And as soon as the curtains close as it were, back to reality they go...

"I cannot believe you did that last night."

"Oh, give me a break. It was only a few hours."

"Yeah, but now my voice is all hoarse and raspy and I have to preach!"

"It was eighty-five degrees! What did you expect?"

"I had the windows open!"

"It was **eighty-five degrees**!"

"With a nice breeze!"

"Are you serious right now? You know I can't sleep with the A/C on! I have to preach, and now my voice is half-gone!"

"Well, if you stop *preaching* to me you might be able to save the other half!"

Yes...It happens. They're right in the thick of a disagreement, and they have to abruptly suspend those feelings to be present with you. In the theatrical world, this would be getting into character.

Or, there's the tension-filled, dreadful drive in silence. The two of you haven't said a word to each other the entire time you've been in the car, and the moment you step out:

"Hey Sugar, God bless you! Is your mama alright? Well, amen."

And all megachurch pastors will readily relate to what I'm about to say. Lady Vernon and I said we would never share this with anyone, but I said it to a room full of pastors, their spouses, and leaders during the teaching that inspired this book and now I'm penning it to the page for you.

When you have 10,000 people all telling you something different, keeping track of their stories can be a formidable task.

A young woman walks up to you. You have no idea who she is, or what she has said to you during a previous exchange. You smile widely, open your arms, and prepare to give her a good godly hug when you notice the expression on her face. Something is terribly wrong.

"Pastor," she says, her voice cracking with sadness. "She didn't make it. Mama died."

Now you have a split second to offer a response, and there is only one appropriate for this interaction.

"Oh my Lord," you say, covering your mouth in disbelief. "Not, Mama. She didn't pull through?"

She shakes her head, "No. The doctors did everything they could."

And in the most dramatic form possible, all you can manage to say is, "What? No!"

She nods, looking you straight in the eyes, a torrent of tears only one blink away.

And just that quickly, you're thrust into the scene, into the moment of grief with her.

"I don't believe this. I'm so sorry."

The woman walks away, still sad, but comforted by her pastor's condolences.

Another time we find ourselves cornered by our conviction to act is when a person approaches us bubbling over, and you have that feeling in your gut that she's about to update you on something she's shared with you before.

"Pastor, I did it!"

The only clue you have is her giddiness, thus, you know it must be something you're supposed to be giddy about too, and you improvise.

"What did I tell you? I knew you would do it! All you had to do was stick with it. Girl, give me a hug!"

And she does, even happier than she was before now that she's gotten her pastor's congratulations.

You've succeeded in meeting the expectation she has for you to celebrate with and be happy for her, and she now feels even more accomplished.

She walks away and as she does, a deep sense of relief washes over you, swilling away the sweat of the moment preceding.

You're all set to greet the next person waiting to speak with you, when you notice "that look" on *their* face...

I said at the beginning of this chapter that if you didn't know your pastor was acting, it's probably because he's very good. That's true.

But by no means am I suggesting that your pastor is acting every time she reacts to something you've told her previously. I would venture to say that these situations are the exception. Ninety-nine percent of the time, we remember what we've been told by whom.

Even those of us with larger congregations have our ways of keeping up with things we're told, so don't go questioning your pastor's authenticity the next time you apprise him of your crisis just because he responds in kind.

Still, when we're called to summon our acting chops, it's the pressure that provokes us. And most often, it works in our favor and yours.

But that is the funny thing about pressure, isn't it?

Former Campbell Soup Company CEO Doug Conant once said that if "necessity is the mother of invention...pressure is the mother of performance."

Think about that.

Pressure—in this case being placed in a situational quandary that requires an immediate response—triggers the need to act on demand. It begets the performance.

With all the other pressures, we've talked about, for the most part, we at least get the luxury of time to prepare. In scenarios like these, the only preparation we've had is the acting we've done in similar, previous scenarios.

I offer the previous examples of the pressures other pastors and I are under to perform in jest—but make no mistake about it. It is a crucial part of what I do. Of what your pastor does. And as with the other pressures, there is no way to get around it. It comes with the job.

I hope that I haven't given you the impression that the reason for putting on this little charade is to appeal to our flair for the dramatic or hone our stagecraft for a foray in theater later in life.

This pressure, or requirement to act spontaneously in an appropriate manner for myriad situations, is not *merely* the pull to perform. To leave it at that would be to downplay the real purpose of the performance.

I could've even rephrased the wording and remained true to my Ps.

It is the *pressure to be present*, and the root of this stress stems from our recognition of your need to connect.

When you tell us your stories, whether it's a change you've experienced, a challenge you face, or a child who's making choices you don't understand, you inform us because you have an expectation. You want us to remember you in our prayers, as an individual, not just as a part of the collective (which is why I often respond to such requests by praying on the spot). You want us to get in the fight with you, if only in spirit. You want us to think about you, to share in your pain and rejoice in your perseverance.

And rightfully so. That's what we're here for. It's why we've been called to shepherd you. It's what we *desire* to do. So, when you approach us on the weekends to give us an earful about what's going on in your life and relationships, we want to hear about it.

In those situations, irrespective of how tired we are or how many other things are running through our minds, we deny ourselves the privilege to attune to our personal needs and instead listen attentively to yours so that we can respond in a way that ministers to what matters most to you in that moment.

When you come back to us to bring us up-to-speed on a predicament you were facing and we can't readily recall what you could possibly be talking about, our choice to act is our way of being present for you, of giving you the same sensitivity and consideration we gave you when you first approached us about the issue.

And lest you think otherwise, beloved, our acting is not an artifice of affirmation, nor is the intent to deceive in a way that is harmful. It is sincere, our heartfelt attempt to be present with you in whatever you feel, wherever you are in life.

After all, the alternative would be to say, "Son, I haven't the slightest idea what you're talking about. You did what now?"

Imagine the look on his face, or worse yet, the feeling in his chest.

He spent five minutes last month telling you all about his biggest fear, something he'd never shared with anyone. You prayed with him and gave him advice that he followed through on. He comes back to be accountable to you (because you told him to), and you don't even remember what he said...? Do you even care? Did you ever care?

Of course you do and you did, but Godspeed convincing him of your concern.

No matter how much you try to explain all the reasons why you don't remember, they'll all sound like excuses to him. You can and should apologize, and he may accept, but he'll still likely to be offended at your perceived slight and become another broken soul, hurt by his church.

One wrong word or reaction from a pastor can change a person's life. Bishop Joey tells me that I shouldn't regret anything I've done given that I did what I thought was best based on what I knew.

But if I were to regret anything in life, it would be underestimating the power of my influence.

Humor has always been a part of who I am, but on occasion, unbeknownst to me at the time, it has been to my detriment, and others'. I've joked with people, who later quit the church because of what I said. It saddens me even now when I think about it. I only meant to share a laugh...talk about an epic fail.

Like most pastors, I'm more relaxed in the presence of staff than I am in front of the entire congregation. And typically, the smaller the room, the more comfortable I am. But that has sometimes come at a cost.

I've said things freely in my office thinking I could loosen up a little, and ended up wounding someone with my words.

Because you're reading this book, you now have insight and information that the average lay member doesn't, so if your pastor slips up and says something that offends you, you might be more inclined to let him off the hook.

Even if you are not able to experientially identify, if I've done a decent job, you at least understand what your pastor is up against.

But most people don't, therefore, they're not likely to give their pastor a pass if he forgets a meaningful detail of their lives, tells a joke that hits a sore spot because of a personal issue they have, or mentions something in casual conversation that insults them in some way. Hence, the pressure to perform.

Yes, we're pastors and conceivably have a considerable threshold for handling life's burdens, perhaps more than those who don't share our mantle. But, we do have our limits too.

We're careful not to show them and we'd never use our platform as a place to vent our personal frustrations; however, there are times when we just don't have it all together, and rather than not show up—*What! Pastor took a personal day? On a Sunday?!*—we step into our starring roles.

Your pastor has children who weigh on his heart just like yours do. He has a wife who needs him and sometimes feels neglected. He has aging parents who depend on him to be there when he calls.

And as a woman, first ladies and female senior pastors have another kind of performance pressure that her male counterparts don't: her attire.

If she dresses too nice, she'll be accused of showing off. If she doesn't dress nice enough, she's embarrassing the church.

She's relatively young, so she wants to wear clothing that reflects her youthfulness, but she has to be careful to never appear "sexy." She does not want men lusting after her.

She's thinking of the women who are younger than her, who look up to her and notice her style, and want them to see that she's fly enough to relate to them, but at the same time, she doesn't want them to think she's looking for attention.

Sometimes, your pastor feels discouraged and isolated in his feelings. He's irritated that there are things happening in his life that are beyond his control.

It doesn't matter that he's preoccupied with a situation he's been trying to sort through all week. He'd better be able to snap out of it when duty calls, because the one time a person looking for their pastor's loving embrace walks up to him and he inadvertently fails to acknowledge their presence, or speaks to them in haste so he isn't late for the next service, all the rejection they've ever felt comes rushing back at once.

It's important for Lady Vernon and I that we stand and hug every person we can who wants a touch from us. We consider it one of the most important things we do.

I try to listen and give a thoughtful response to every person who approaches me, no matter how many there are waiting in line to speak with me; however, it's just not always possible.

But for the one who felt like they needed me that day and I wasn't there for them in the way they expected, in their mind, I have failed them. They walk away grieved by what they perceive was a snub.

My wife and I have been at churches—some with fewer, some with more members than we have—where the pastor jettisons the stage the moment he's done preaching. He doesn't even think about sticking around to see who needs what.

I don't think that's the best way of handling people who pay your salary, but the irony is, because he doesn't do it, his members don't really expect him to, and don't feel that he loves them any less because he doesn't.

Without this expectation to fulfill, people don't feel hurt or slighted when he leaves without hugging or talking to them.

Well, because I *do* make it a habit of loving on my people, they expect it, so on occasion, if I can't get to a person who's been waiting all week to talk to me, they're upset. You may even call this the "pressure of pastoral care," and it's not limited to these kinds of interactions. It is an area where we fail to meet the expectations of those we've been called to cover in their time of pain or joy, anxiety or elation, trials or triumphs. James Taylor says it this way:

One other area of failure is worth identifying; that of failure in pastoral care. For a pastor there is no more distressing area of failure. We can see the evidence of what we believe to be our failure in the ruined lives, broken homes and wounded spirits of the people we claim to be looking after. Neither the evidence of our failure nor the questions our failure stimulates easily disappear. Months, if not years after, we are still asking 'Could I have handled it differently? Could I have done more? How responsible am I for the present situation?'

It goes without saying, too, that there are some sheep intent on straying and, no matter how energetic and devoted the shepherd, they will do so. Who has failed here, the shepherd or the sheep? No doubt the shepherd will blame himself...[15]

It's a bit of a catch-22, because even though I'm trying, there are times that I feel as if I'm still losing.

But alas, such is the life I've chosen, and I'll continue to keep loving, hugging, and performing because it's what I've been called to do, and the ones who walk away wounded may need a touch more than the ones who don't.

---

[15] (Taylor, 2004 p. 64)

FIVE | **THE PRESSURE TO PROVIDE**

Your pastor has an obligation to be as much like Jesus as he possibly can. He should love like Jesus, lead like Jesus, and liberate like Jesus, but, unless he plans to stay single, abstain from sex, forego having children, and be dead by thirty-three, he probably shouldn't live like Jesus.

Now, when most *pastors* say they want to live like Jesus, they're referring to the values and principles Jesus taught, showed, and lived by, not necessarily the lifestyle he chose.

However, others, critical of how much some pastors earn for a living, mean exactly that—that all pastors should live a self-sacrificing life like Jesus did. They shouldn't have six figure salaries ever, and if they do, they should give away all but enough to cover necessities.

This is pejorative thinking at best; parochial reasoning at worst, and if the leaders of the church don't understand this, the church at large doesn't stand a chance.

Much of this criticism has come in response to sensational media headlines flaunting some pastors' affluent standard of living absent of any context. The picture is presented in a way that primes the observer to believe a wealthy pastor is using Jesus to con poor people out of their money so that they can enjoy fancy cars and multi-million-dollar mansions. Slanderous opinions are then formed and spread and suddenly, any pastor who drives a nice car or earns more than average is a crook.

To be fair, there have been a few unfortunate cases where pastors have been caught misusing church funds. However, instances like these are the exception, and it's wrong to make sweeping generalizations about all pastors based on the broad brushstrokes of zealous faultfinders.

Neither Jesus nor Paul are appropriate biblical models for determining how much today's pastor should earn. They led very different lives than the ones we do today and without wives and children, didn't have to worry about others depending on them for provision.

The ascetic framework is only fair if your pastor has chosen to live as a monk or priest. Otherwise, it's erroneous to anachronistically apply first century text to twenty-first century context.

Jesus said to Pilate in John 18:37, "...To this end was I born, for this cause I came into the world, that I should bear witness unto the truth..." His assignment was to die by age thirty-three so that we could live eternally.

The choice to work in ministry for free or for very little in a pastoral position is a personal one. If a person has determined that their lot in life is to work for no or very little pay, or to give most of his earnings away, it is likely that he has arranged other means of supporting himself and his family.

For example, pastor and bestselling author Rick Warren, is reportedly worth twenty-five million dollars. He's written several books and founded various ministries that have all done well. He chooses to donate ninety-percent of his income and live on ten.

In Rick's case, he has made a comfortable living using his other gifts in addition to serving as pastor at Saddleback, thereby positioning himself to be able to live on a fraction of his salary. Not many pastors—or working people period for that matter—are this fortunate.

But the point here is that for him to be *able* to give away as much as he does, he must receive it first.

The big question is, how much should a pastor be compensated? While there are various factors that affect how much a pastor can receive in salary, I believe that he or she should be compensated based on their assignment.

Let's unpack that.

If he has a wife and small children, then without question, his personal assignment is to take care of them, to provide for their needs the best he can. I Timothy 5:8 says, "But if anyone does not provide for his own, and especially for those of his household, he has denied the faith and is worse than an unbeliever."

I think it's clear how important it is for a husband to honor his responsibility to those who depend on him.

Considering, where should he live? Among those whom he covers?

While that may sound appealing in theory, imagine how often people would invade his and his family's privacy because they "need" something if he's that easily accessible. People would knock on his door simply because they could.

As his influence and audience grows, they'd begin to tell others, "That's where Pastor Jackson lives. Yep, right across the street from me. I can see when they come and go from my front window. Mm-hm. Oh, look! Here comes Lady Jackson now. Let me catch her before she leaves. I've been meaning to talk to her..."

I'm not telling you what I think; I'm telling you what I know, because I've experienced it.

The pressure of the fame and celebrity that comes with being a prominent pastor is undesirable and unforgiving. Very few of the renowned pastors I know want the kind of attention that they get. But the flipside would be to get no attention, and if he isn't receiving any attention he may not be sharing the Gospel in a way that draws attention, and that isn't good either.

Pastors often become well-known because of their presence on national television. But nowadays, the way technology and social media have changed the way we communicate, even if a church budget doesn't afford a pastor a ministry on TV, it's easier than ever to share the Good News of Jesus Christ. As such, some pastors become insta-celebrities simply because of their social media savvy in spreading God's word.

Trust me, it is ideal for him to live in a gated, private, or secluded community, where even if his neighbors do know him and what he does for a living, they don't care enough to want to drop by for a visit.

Your pastor needs and deserves solitude and space, regardless of whether they have a spouse and children, but especially if they do. Because he is not likely to get it anywhere else, his home needs to be a retreat, a place he can feel at peace and apart from the pressures of people and ministry.

Arguably, pastors have the most important job in the world.

When I was ousted from my first ministry, the leaders also confiscated the car they had given me, with my son Ray's car seat still in the back. One of them drove it away, while Lady Vernon and I watched, powerless in the moment. The others stood in the cliques and laughed, all while local news cameras filmed, capturing every second of our misfortune, so that they could later report my demise to hundreds of thousands of families during the dinner hour on Sunday evening.

It was, hands down, the worst day of my life.

Sometime after that, I purchased a Ford Explorer. It was all I could afford. It was primarily for Lady Vernon, but since it was the only vehicle we had, we shared it. This meant that on most Sundays and Wednesdays (unless I wanted to run the risk of being late), I'd have to hitch a ride or walk to church so that she would have a way to get there with our three small children.

By this time, I had started The Word Church, and we were holding services in a high school about a mile and a half from where we lived.

We had about a thousand members, and a young pro football player, Corey Fuller of the Cleveland Browns, had begun attending my church. I will never forget Corey, nor what he said to me one afternoon.

He said, "How is it that I catch footballs for a living, and make millions of dollars, and you're changing my life and the city of Cleveland, and have to walk to church?"

He went on, "I have a Benz. Tomorrow, we're going to get one for you."

Corey understood what many people who judge pastors for their wealth or material possessions do not.

There are people who do work that is far less significant than the work we do, and make millions of dollars for it. Shouldn't a pastor be able to enjoy nice things too? Is he unspiritual if he's rewarded for his work with memorable life experiences and generous comforts? We'll get back to these questions in a moment.

I'm not sure if he was even aware of it at the time, but in effect, Corey was living out Galatians 6:6, "The one who is taught the word is to share all good things with the one who teaches him."

Pastors need money to live of course, but that's not all they need. Anyone who shares or has ever had to share a car with their spouse knows how taxing and difficult it can be to try to navigate each person's responsibilities outside of the home with only one vehicle, especially when you have kids.

But sometimes, it is what it is. You can't afford insurance, maintenance, and payments on two cars, so you do what you have to do. It's what Lady Vernon and I did—walked, asked for rides, borrowed other people's cars, or just stayed home—until Corey came along and blessed our life with that Benz.

If you're able to be a blessing to your pastor or their spouse, particularly if you know there is an area of lack in their life, do what you can to share "all good things with them."

Maybe they've been grinding for months without a break and you know they need some rest. Send them on a life-changing vacation.

Perhaps your pastor is into sports. Treat him and his wife with tickets to their favorite team's next home game.

Maybe you've heard her talk about how much she loves to listen to audiobooks because she can listen to them while in the car or doing other things. Gift her a subscription to an audiobook service so she can listen to whatever she wants, whenever she wants.

We already talked about the pressure she's under to dress well. Get her a gift card to her preferred retailer so she can update her wardrobe.

Now, don't start cooking chicken, baking cakes, and bombarding them after service with aluminum foil wrapped goods unless they have personally asked you for that. As a rule of thumb, stick to non-food items.

The point is, not only is it thoughtful to shower your pastor with gifts, it's scriptural. You'll be honoring God and your man and woman of God when you do so, and your pastor will be encouraged by your generosity.

Now, back to the questions I asked earlier in reference to what your pastor should be able to experience or enjoy.

If a church is doing well and appropriately allocating its resources, what percentage should the pastor—the one who's running the whole thing—be entitled to? If he started the church, how much of the church's revenue should he earn? One percent, two percent, ten?

If under his preaching, leadership, and vision, the church becomes a multimillion dollar organization, what does he deserve for his ingenuity and acumen?

Think about this for a second: In any other profession, if he grew a business from nothing into a profitable, self-sustaining enterprise, he'd be considered one of the foremost business minds of our time. We'd hail him a genius.

But because he's a pastor, we call him a pimp.

Steve Jobs, even in death, is still heralded as one of the most brilliant intellects of our time, and will be remembered throughout history for the way his ideas changed our lives—genius.

Howard Schultz took a local coffee shop and turned it into a household brand—genius.

Oprah, the first black woman to become a TV correspondent in Nashville, now a multimedia icon—genius.

John Paul Mitchell—genius.

Sara Blakely—genius.

Billionaires, each one of them. And rightfully, they deserve the recognition and the acclaim they receive for being frontrunners in their respective industries and for what they accomplished without racks on racks on racks or sizeable investments from venture capitalists.

Why is it different with pastors?

Like the billionaires I referenced, my wife and I too started with nothing. No cameras, microphones, screens, instruments, equipment; not even a building, and by the grace and favor of God, we built The Word Church into what it is today.

The church employs close to a hundred people. Part of our campus doubles as a sports complex, of which some of the activity is for-profit, with three basketball courts, two soccer fields, and a billiards hall, where athletes of all ages come to play and compete. We've given away several cars and homes, and millions of dollars in outreach over the years.

If the church brings in eight or nine million dollars, should we receive one of them? Is that far too much?

But a professional baseball player, who only throws a ball once every five days, can earn a salary of $215 million over seven years? Granted, most sports teams are part of billion dollar conglomerates, which is where they get the funds to pay players' lofty salaries, and pastoral salaries come from tithes and offerings.

Laying aside the technical differences, however, let's consider the implications and apply the thinking.

How are we okay with athletes making substantial sums of money, playing games no less, when pastors are conducting serious spiritual business, saving and changing lives, and we decry *the very idea* of them being well-off?

Your pastor helps men and women become better husbands and wives, stronger fathers and mothers. He gives hope to people who were lost, confused, and depressed. He's inspired thousands to pursue education, create a vision for their lives, and repair broken relationships.

He creates opportunities for people to get jobs, feeds the hungry, and partners with local schools to fill in gaps where district budgets fall short. He offers counseling and spiritual guidance services to the community. He continues to strengthen morale in the city by providing a place where all are welcome to come and receive the love and message of Jesus Christ.

This is not worth just as much (or more) than the recreational utility of sporting events?

I'm not picking on athletes. I'm a huge sports fan, and I understand how professional sports teams can inspire hometown pride and provide a marginal boost to a city's tourism and consumerism.

I just want you to see how the logic in our culture about who should be paid what or how much we're willing to pay to whom is skewed in favor of what bring us entertainment value or yields superficial returns on our monetary contributions.

Think about it. Without blinking, you'll pay $60 for a ticket to see someone dribble and shoot a basketball...but *we're* the pimps? Who's really hustling you?

We don't tend to see it that way, though do we?

Here's why: because we got what we wanted out of the experience. We enjoyed ourselves. We got a chance to kick it with our families for a while. Our kids got to feel what's it's like to watch a game live.

Furthermore, we're grown, it's our money, we earned it, and we can spend it how we want to. If we choose to spend $50 on a concert ticket, that's our business, right?

So, why don't "they" say this about tithing?

Conceivably, when you give to your local church, you receive something meaningful in return, not the least of which are God's heavenly promises and blessings here on earth. Further, while most of what we spend our money on is fleeting in the larger scheme of life, the benefits of tithing are eternal.

So, I ask again, how much should a pastor make? Would you really feel better if he's broke? If he makes less than you? Is he more spiritual because he can't afford to take a vacation? Is his piety measured by his proximity to the poverty line, meaning the paltrier his pay, the more pious he is? Is he more like Jesus because he lacks?

His lights are cut off but he's so Christ-like.

Surely, we can't be this shallow!

Yet, sadly, many people are.

A few years ago, a prominent pastor in Atlanta opened a second campus in New York, holding services on Saturday night. Thousands of people show up every week, presumably to hear the love and message of Jesus Christ.

His services on Sunday in Atlanta were filled as well.

To those of you who take issue with pastors having private jets, I have one question: How do you suggest he get back and forth between campuses when there are no red-eye flights on the east coast? Should he drive through the night to make sure he's back by Sunday morning?

I don't know him personally, so I can't speak to his private life, say that I agree with his theological position on every issue, or validate the way he chooses to lead his ministry.

But from a practical standpoint, without a private jet to transport him, how else would he be able to be in both places at the time he needs to be?

This is why I believe that your assignment dictates your need. You may not need a private jet if you're a plumber, electrician, mechanic, or administrator, but if you're a pastor who has to get to multiple cities in the span of a few hours, well you just might. This same pastor was quoted as saying that he would gladly take a commercial plane, but none of them fly his schedule.

I cover some four-hundred pastors across the country—a calling I take very seriously—who call and ask me to renew their vows, dedicate their buildings, and the like. I'm often limited in when I can go because of the lack of flight options that would get me there and back in time for me to still meet my own vocational and personal responsibilities at home.

It's the twenty-first century. At the time of this writing, I am forty-six years old. I went to school eight years and earned three degrees. I've been doing one thing since I was child. I've loved one woman and have never been involved in any kind of scandal. Our church grows at a rate of about two-hundred people per month. I've worked and continue to work to be good at my craft.

What is fair compensation for my diligence and labor? Just enough to silence or satisfy my critics?

Some people don't care what pastors make, and while they've been faithful churchgoers since the start of the ministry, they've never put any money in his hand.

But they've spent money on family members who have hurt them and who consistently mismanage their money.

I'm not picking on them either, nor am I criticizing their financial choices. Quite the opposite. I'm highlighting the fact that we spend our money the way we want, and sometimes in places where we know the return won't be equitable. It's our choice.

What is the issue then, when a person believes that the man and woman of God deserve to be well paid? Why do people trip if a man or woman says they contribute faithfully to their local church to make sure, among other things, their pastors are compensated with a healthy salary?

Most people who don't sow into their pastor's lives regularly or even sporadically don't because they have never been taught or told why it's important to do so. It's not something they think about, but it has nothing to do with a lack of consideration or concern for their pastor's wellbeing. They simply don't know. I'm hoping that changes with you.

I don't lose any sleep any more over what I make. I'm at peace with it because I know the value of what I do. I'll take the criticism because I understand what my critics don't—that I can't be poor or struggling to pay my own bills and preach with confidence that God will provide all my members' needs; that I can't give to the needy if I'm needy myself; that it takes money to help people, to influence policy and legislation, to put my kids through college without burdening them with debt; that I can't focus on ministry if I'm concerned about how I'm going to take care of my family.

And here's something you should be concerned about as a person who looks to your pastor to provide spiritual nourishment; if he's preoccupied with figuring out how he's going to pay his bills, your servings are going to get skimpy.

Think about times in your life when lack of money was an issue. Remember how difficult it was to concentrate on other things? Think about the mental energy you consumed trying to determine where you were going to get the extra money you needed to pay for that unexpected car repair, medical bill, or flooded basement?

Your pastor is human too. He's spiritual, but he has an emotional side as well. There are times when anxiety wells up in his spirit because he has a responsibility to provide and if he can't, he feels he's failing his family. Now, he's saddled with stress.

Trust me. He cannot focus on preaching, praying for you, ministering, or leading when money is an issue. He's not going to say it, though. That's why I'm telling you.

At this juncture, I encourage you to speak life, faith, and favor over your man and woman of God. Pray for their prosperity. The next time you see them or even when you think about them, declare blessings over their life—and put some money in their hand.

I'm sure that the passion with which I've discussed this topic does not elude your inner ear. Everything I've written here is personal to me, but this pressure—the pressure to provide—is particularly disconcerting because I know so many struggling pastors who are giving all they have but are still underpaid (when they don't have to be).

Forget what you heard; most pastors are not rolling in dough. Most pastors are making a less than comfortable salary. "The reality is that most of the some 400,000 pastors in America are not overpaid; indeed many are underpaid."[16]

You've read my personal take—let me also give you some biblical backing.

I Timothy 5:17-18 (NLT) says, "[17]Elders who do their work well should be respected and paid well, especially those who work hard at both preaching and teaching. [18]For the Scripture says, 'You must not muzzle an ox to keep it from eating as it treads out the grain.' And in another place, 'Those who work deserve their pay!'"

You may be more familiar with the New American Standard version, which says, "[17]The elders who rule well are to be considered worthy of double honor, especially those who work hard at preaching and teaching. [18]For the Scripture says, 'You shall not muzzle the ox while he is threshing,' and 'The laborer is worthy of his wages.'"

The scriptures here refer to financial support, and while "double honor" does leave room for subjective interpretation, the emphasis and inference here is that those who rule well **and** preach and teach the word should be compensated generously.

Professor and theologian Wayne Grudem sees it this way:

> The connection of verses 17 and 18 shows us how highly Paul valued the ministry of the gospel. He says, in effect, "So if even these deserve a fair wage, then how much is deserved by the one who works all the time in the highest and most important calling God gives? Certainly, his work is worth at least twice what other people get!" [17]

He concedes that scripture does not stipulate exactly whose salary pastors should get double of, but attributes this lack of specificity to the fact that "it probably was not necessary in a society where the wage structure was much less complex than ours."

He goes on to muse that the jobs that we should compare our pastors' to are the ones considered most important in society; CEOs, attorneys, doctors, "people who often earn double what ordinary people earn." He also denotes that while the Bible says pastors are "worthy" of double honor, it's understood that some churches don't have the budget to pay a high salary. Still:

> "...it says he is "worthy" of it. How wise Scripture is! Perhaps there are some churches so small they can't pay a pastor much at all. God does not command them to pay their pastor twice as much as the average pay in their community. He just says the pastor deserves that much, and that is something the church should remember as it plans and grows.[18]

I agree with Grudem's idea that though a church may not be in a position to pay a pastor the salary he deserves, getting fiscally fit so that you can should be as important as any other church missions.

Where I would venture further is on the point that "elders who rule well" are the ones the Bible says are worthy of double honor.

That means as a pastor, you're administrating, leading, loving, casting vision, discipling, touching people, and prepared to preach. You're listening to your members and walking in humility before them. Even if you were rich before you started pastoring, if their contributions help pay your salary now, you and your spouse should engage your members with grateful dispositions.

One last thing. You can and should consult with a financial professional with experience in church accounting to look at your church's finances for specific guidance on how you should allocate your resources. I'd recommend looking into the services of Justin Osteen, Pastor Joel Osteen's brother. He has a consultation business that provides budget analysis and customized, meticulously detailed executive compensation reports for churches and other nonprofit organizations, regardless of size.

Most accounting professionals advise that in a healthy, growing church, where finances are being managed appropriately, staffing salaries should account from somewhere between thirty to fifty-five percent of the budget.

---

[16] (Rainer, 2012)

[17] (What The Bible Says About Paying Your Pastor, 1981)

[18] Ibid.

SIX | **HOW YOU CAN HELP ALLEVIATE PRESSURE: PARTICIPATE**

Lessening your pastor's pressure requires one thing… your participation.

The pressures that I've explained in this book inhere in pastoring—they are inescapable and inextricably linked to the call.

Nonetheless, now that you understand your pastor's pressures, it is my prayer that you will do whatever is in your power to lighten his burdens, so that the strain of his pressures doesn't strip him of his resolve and render him less effective in the one thing he's been called to do above all else.

HONOR

The first and most significant thing you can do to participate in the lessening of your pastor's load is honor him. Praise Jesus, honor your pastor.

No one likes to hang out where they don't feel honor.

You may wonder, "Why don't my kids ever climb in bed and hang out with me?"

If you're a parent who constantly yells, fusses, or shames your kids, they'll love you, but will spend most of their time in their room or somewhere out of your presence to avoid your attitude.

If you complain about what they have or haven't done; if you criticize and bark orders more than you compliment and affirm, the answer is, they don't feel honored.

Contrary to popular belief, men don't go to strip clubs solely or even mostly because they want to see half-naked women dancing. They go to strip clubs because they want to feel affirmed, admired, and appreciated.

Every man knows the scantily clad pretender prancing in front of him is being disingenuous when she tells him how fine he is or how much she wants him, but he doesn't care. He'd rather hear her lie, than go home and hear his wife's truth, because the stripper makes him feel honored.

Apparently, men aren't the only ones who need honor.

My dog, Marley, slept in the basement for the first time after a two-week stint of being overlooked. We'd brought a puppy, Prissy, into our home and like a new baby, she got all the attention. Marley went completely unnoticed. After

102

several futile attempts to engage us, he finally retreated in defeat to the basement.

Now if a dog aches for honor and a sense of belonging, how much more do we as human beings need it?

That said, for any pastor reading this, honor goes both ways. Respect your leaders as fellow brothers and sisters in Christ. While they may not be senior pastors, they are still God's children, and He honors us simply because we belong to Him. We don't earn His honor; He gives it liberally, so who are we to withhold it from anyone?

When you have to discipline or reprimand one of your staff because someone dropped a ball, choose your words thoughtfully. Leave them with their dignity intact.

Bishop Joey told me years ago that whenever I'm giving directives to those who work under me to sprinkle them with, "ma'am" and "sir." The reason is simple. When people feel respected and valued, and their service acknowledged, they feel better about what they do. When they feel better about what they do, it'll show in their productivity. They'll labor with more pride and passion.

I followed Bishop's advice and saw and felt a difference in my chemistry with my staff immediately.

> "Honor is the atmosphere in which the people of God become their best." It comes from a heart of

excellence, is how we display value, and is one of the clearest expressions of love...Honor brings out the greatness that lies hidden."[19]

Whenever I come out onstage to speak, my church stands. I have never instructed them to do so. But they do.

Sometimes when I walk out, it's dark because there's a video playing on the screens, but even in the dark, when they see my silhouette, they rise to their feet and I think, *Man, that's honor.*

When a judge walks into a room, we stand. For the pledge of allegiance, time-honored tradition compel us to stand. It's a display of respect that until recently, few people ever questioned.

Standing denotes a person or a custom is important and if you as the leader don't set the tone, no one else will know.

If your church isn't in the habit of standing when your pastor walks onto the stage, pulpit, or in a room, suggest to your fellow staff in ministry that you start, and the next time the opportunity presents itself, show him that you esteem him. It only takes a few to set the atmosphere; the rest of the church will follow suit when they see what you're doing. If anyone is deserving of this simple expression of honor, your pastor is.

The next time he's preaching and he makes a point, be the first to jump to your feet and encourage him with an 'amen.'

When he calls for an offering, get to the basket quickly. If you don't have anything to give, borrow something and get there.

These small but significant gestures will make him feel honored and respected.

This brings to mind a movie I watched last year starring Michael Douglas called, *The American President*.

As a pastor, I always view movies with storylines about people in positions of authority through a leadership lens. Rather than just be entertained, I try to glean principles that I can apply in my work, and in this movie, there were quite a few. You'd be well served to watch it yourself.

But aside from that, in the movie, Michael Douglas (Andrew Shepherd) plays the role of President of the United States, and his best friend is his chief of staff. They've known each other for years. They went to college together and worked side-by-side on the campaign trail.

They're shooting pool one day, and the best friend says to him, "Mr. President..."

Before he can finish, Douglas's character says, "You've known me thirty years. Don't call me Mr. President when we're alone. Just call me Andrew."

His best friend answers, "Yes Sir, Mr. President."

It didn't matter to the best friend that they'd known each other over half their lives. Andrew Shepherd's rank came with a title, President of the United States, and out of honor for the former, he called him by the latter.

In other words, his best friend didn't want to be too common with him. *You're not "my boy," you're my president, and even when you let your hair down, I'll still be professional.*

If you're close enough to your pastor that he feels comfortable joking or speaking casually in front of or with you, allow him that space—he probably needs it.

But be mindful of the boundaries that delineate the relationship. He's still your pastor. Don't be robotic or mechanical, fake laughing at things that aren't funny, nodding at everything, or responding in monotonous one-word answers because that's weird and will make both of you uncomfortable.

Just use your discretion. Joke a little, participate in the conversation, but know when to reel it back in.

Because they're so cool, sometimes it feels like your pastor could be your boy and your first lady could be your girl, but the reality is, they're not. They are who they are and it's important that you maintain and protect those relational perimeters so that others who observe your interaction with them don't get the wrong idea.

In the White House, loyal staffers utter the phrase, "I serve at the pleasure of the President." It is a statement that underlines a pledge to obey directives in deference to the President's will or wishes. It carries the idea of unwavering allegiance.

How are government employees more loyal to their superior than the church is to theirs?

When I'm with Bishop Joey, I abdicate the celebrity that comes with who I am as much as possible. I'm just a son when he's around. I carry his bags and serve him however I can. I tell his regular assistants that they can relax when I'm present, because I'm there to serve at his pleasure.

Your pastor needs to know you have his back—that you are resolute in your loyalty to him.

In WRYC?, Jennifer gave a bit of advice to pastors about the people who they choose to surround themselves with, but every person who serves in any capacity, especially those in key roles can learn something from this:

> Your team members, in most of your positions but especially these, need to be mini versions of you.

Walking, talking, sensing, replicas. In the context of your ministry, when they speak, it sounds like your voice. When they listen, they hear with your heart. When they act, they behave with your integrity. When they think, they deliberate with the things that are important to you in mind.

Of course, they are individuals with their own awareness, inclinations, and preferences, but when they work for you, they appropriate their intelligence to serve you and your ministry's goals.

So, what does this mean for you as the leader? A lot of pressure to be right—not perfect—but right.

If you've got character issues, that's going to drip down to your team.

If you've got control issues, that's also going to drip down to your team.

If you've got insecurity issues, you'll be surrounded by "yes" people who have learned clandestine ways to appeal to those insecurities to stay in your good graces—and the opinions of "yes" people are at best incredible; at worst misleading.

If you lead with an iron fist, people will operate out of their fear of you or of losing their jobs [or positions], not because they believe in you, and that kind of intimidation is damaging on many levels.

Your position calls for the highest level of conscientiousness, of your moral, ethical, and spiritual cognizance. If you want mini versions of you, be an extraordinary original.[20]

SERVE

Your pastor needs you operating in your role every weekend. He depends on you. Barring emergency, try not to miss the days you're supposed to serve. He's counting on you to help him build the ministry.

In smaller churches, it's more obvious when someone is missing in ministry than in larger ministries because there are no backups. There are only a handful of faithful volunteers; if three people are out, it's going to affect the flow of service.

You are an integral part of what he's trying to get done whether you usher, greet, sing in the choir, or clean up. Get involved, get connected, and rally others to do the same.

A pastor can only be as good as his support system. If the right people aren't in place or doing their jobs, it's going to bring growth to a halt.

And yes, your service, even your volunteer service is a job. If you do anything at your church to benefit the Kingdom, whether you get paid for it or not, you are staff.

Care about what you do. Be consistent. Be conscientious. Be constructive.

PROTECT

If you're a staff person, your pastor trusts you implicitly. He believes you're going to protect him and his family from gossip, criticism, false accusations, and the like. He expects that you would never engage in such activity, and that if you hear others participating in this kind of negativity, especially others in leadership, you'll bring it to his attention, if appropriate, or to the attention of your superior.

Lady Vernon and I are fortunate in that this hasn't been an issue for us in seventeen years. We lead with candor and encourage it, so people conduct themselves according to the culture we've created, which doesn't lend itself to a whole lot of complaints, criticism, or cowardly conversations behind our backs.

When people do have a grievance, they'll walk up to me after service, and respectfully tell me how they feel. I welcome their honesty.

One that I've heard a few times is, "Pastor, I joined the church a few weeks ago and no one called me."

In these situations and others like it, I immediately apologize.

"I'm so sorry. Because our church is growing so fast we drop the ball sometimes, but you're important to us. Would you give us another chance? As a matter-of-fact, that's the leader over there. Go tell her I sent you, and I want you to join the ministry that dropped you, so you can make sure that this doesn't happen to anyone else."

I also sometimes challenge the person who complains that no one followed up with them.

"Let me ask you a question," I'll say. "Do you think if the person you wanted to speak to had a million dollars for you, you would've found them?"

They'll look at me puzzled for a second, and then the light bulb comes on.

"If serving in ministry is important to you, fight to get to whoever you need to get to. The fact that no one called you is exactly why we need your help."

Usually, they respond in the affirmative, and walk away feeling heard, understood, and encouraged.

When you hear someone criticize your pastor, first lady, or a staff member, stand up for him or her behind the scenes. Be a voice of encouragement to your pastor's family when negativity strikes.

Your pastor will face some criticism; it comes with the territory.

> Pastors are public figures, and thus big targets for criticism in the church and community. What members may not know is how much this criticism affects the pastor's family. Social media has given a voice to every moron in society, and every word can be a weapon which causes collateral damage in the pastor's home. [21]

I don't recommend that you intervene in every instance of social media shade directed at your pastor or try to tell some random person off because they disagree with something he said or did, but I do want you to be conscientious of how it affects him when he catches wind of it.

I try to stay away from comment sections and have someone from my tech team handle most of my social media. But I don't live in a vacuum, and so I hear stuff sometimes, and it hurts. Your pastor is no different. He is neither immune nor invincible, and often, he's more hurt because of how discouraging it can be to his family, especially his children.

But if you witness a leader doing this, in person, on the phone, on social media, or otherwise, tell the appropriate person as soon as possible. When someone condemns or criticizes your pastor publicly, it's clear where their loyalty does *not* lie. If you don't bring this duplicity to your pastor's attention, your loyalty can be called into question too.

In fact, if possible, make the person aware that as a leader, talking about your pastor behind his back is not a practice your church condones or permits, and that you're bound by your own conviction to say something.

Do more than just defend your pastor, because the reality is, once the culture shifts within the congregation that won't be a concern. Speak highly of him when it's opportune at church, at work, at home, on social media, wherever you're comfortable. But don't overdo it, so as not to invite more unnecessary scrutiny or criticism.

For example, don't say, "My pastor can out-preach any pastor in the world." That's foolish.

Say instead, "The message my pastor preached today gave me so much life!" If there's a clip on YouTube or on your church's website and if you think it'll help someone else, share it.

You should also protect your pastor and the first family physically, with armed security, particularly if you are a part of a more visible ministry.

It's sad, no doubt, but we live in a world where deranged people may hear something your pastor said on TV or on social media and because they disagree, come to your church with the intent to do your pastor or your fellow members harm.

We've all heard the stories, not unlike the one in Charleston, South Carolina where a self-proclaimed white supremacist walked in and massacred nine innocent people, including the senior pastor, former senator Clementa Pinckney.

There should be at least one person on the pastor and his family who is licensed to carry. A lay person does not need to be a police officer to legally carry a weapon. He can get a concealed carry permit and be within the confines of the law to protect his pastor, and others if necessary.

The larger your church, the more security there should be, and they should be present at every service.

GIVE

We've discussed at length your pastor's pressure to provide. When you give systematically (tithes and offering) and spontaneously (seeds, gifts), you help your pastor to meet his financial obligations and alleviate the associated stresses of paying bills.

Giving has both biblical and practical implications, earthly and heavenly blessings. It is an expression of both your obedience to and faith in God, and demonstrates your commitment to the Kingdom and Body of Christ.

But take it a step further. Advocate for your pastor. Encourage others to be faithful givers. Consider it your personal responsibility to make sure your pastor is well taken care of.

PRAY

Your pastor needs your prayers, much like you need his. He needs you to cover him. He's fighting battles you will never know, spiritual and otherwise. He needs you to pray for him peace, his perseverance, and his personal struggles.

When you do (and I hope you do it often), tell him that you're doing so. The knowledge that others care enough to remember you in prayer is encouraging, and sometimes, is just what you need to get you through the next service, meeting, or counseling session.

You know a great deal of his pressures—intercede for those things specifically. He'll never be able to tell you what internal conflicts he's having; about his brokenness, sadness, or troubles, but these experiences are real and at times overwhelming. You can support him and ease some of his pressure by simply mentioning his name when you pray.

PARTICIPATE BY PROGRESSING

To those of you who are in higher levels of ministry, progress with your pastor. Keep taking your area to another level. It's a sad thing to have to leave people behind because they refuse to grow.

We all have to learn from others, from previous mistakes, and past experiences, but the most useful lessons we learn are those that teach us to find answers on our own.

That's how we keep learning, evolving, creating [and progressing]. Find people who are passionate and who have learned that lesson, and you're well on your way to having a team of rock stars.

Your pastor needs you to embody a deep level of commitment to the ministry and resolve that you will do everything in your power to lessen his burden and free his time by doing your job—whatever that is.

Your pastor can't afford to micromanage his team at every turn, and doesn't have the time nor energy to constantly push you to stay motivated.

Of course, every great leader wants and needs to inspire his followers, but that inspiration should come from being a consistent, consummate example of leadership, not constant surveillance to ensure his subordinates' effectiveness.

If the pastor has to tell a person how to do what he needs them to do in the position he recruited them for, then his efforts (the pastor's that is) are probably concentrated much too low, and is likely weakening his ability to focus on high-level, overarching ministry objectives.

If he's busy telling his administrator how to run the office, who is studying for the weekly message, thinking about next year's budget, or discipling leaders? Every ounce of energy he has to devote to telling staff members how to do their job is an ounce of energy taken away from the things no one can do *but* him.

Don't get me wrong. From time to time, a pastor may observe inefficiency or think of a way to do something better (*he is the pastor, right?*), and at the beginning of any team member's tenure, you'll have to do some teaching and training to get them up to speed.

What I'm referring to is the need for a pastor to always intervene or get involved because a person—plain and simple—just doesn't know how to do their job at the level the position calls for or has become complacent and doesn't work to improve.

Pastors, you should consider your team members' growth in their respective areas one of the most important things you require of them.

Remember, they are the ones running it for you, touching what you can't feel, watching what you don't see, listening to what you don't have time to hear. If you want to increase your ministry's appeal, the people underneath you need to be increasing, in knowledge and experience.

In other words, this aspect of your ministry development is tied to theirs. If they're not getting any better, neither are you.

As gifted as your pastor is, you will hold him back if you, as a staff member, don't stay on top of your area.

Avoid the toxic feeling of complacency, the arrogant, inner narcissist who tells us that we don't need to go above where we are or beyond what we already know.

That's called complacency. Complacency is coasting and coasting is cheating. You can't coast your way through your ministry service any more than you can coast your way through your Christianity.

As a ministry servant, not only are you cheating the ministry when you coast, you're cheating yourself, squandering opportunities for growth and gain. You hold up progress.

Also, you can never get too comfortable when you coast. Coasting is drifting, and only at the pace someone else's wave carries you. You're at the whim of others' efforts, namely your pastor's.

You have no idea when they're going to speed up or change course, and when they do, you're going to get lost or left behind.

Responsible leaders and clear-thinking followers recognize coasting, and when they do, they'll lose interest in what you're offering, or feel like you're not helping them get to their destination. They may even feel like you're dead weight.

When they lose interest, they move on and find someone else to lead or follow so they can keep moving forward.

Coasting might be moving, but it's directionless, meaningless movement.[22]

---

[19] (Johnson, 2014)

[20] (Wainwright, et al., 2014 pp. 173-74)

[21] (Dance, 2017)

[22] (Wainwright, et al., 2014 pp. 30-31, 248, 250)

BIBLIOGRAPHY

Bounds, E. M. 2012. *Power Through Prayer.* Atlanta : Trinity Press, 2012. p. 6 .

—. 2012. *Power Through Prayer.* Atlanta : Trinity, 2012. p. 54.

Dance, Mark. 2017. 7 Things Pastors Wish Their Congregations Knew. *LifeWay.* [Online] April 12, 2017. [Cited: June 3, 2017.] http://www.lifeway.com/pastors/2017/04/12/7-things-pastors-wish-congregations-knew/.

Greene, Robert. 2013. *Mastery.* New York : Penguin, 2013. p. 123.

Houston, Brian. 2015. *Live, Love, Lead: Your Best Is Yet To Come!* New York : FaithWorks, 2015. p. 34.

Johnson, Bill. 2014. *Experience the Impossible: Simple Ways to Unleash Heaven's Power on Earth.* Bloomington : Chosen, 2014. pp. 100-101.

Keller, Tim. 2014. *Prayer: Experiencing Intimacy and Awe With God.* New York : Penguin, 2014. p. 22.

Maxwell, John C. 2011. *The 360 Degree Leader: Developing Your Influence from Anywhere in The Organization.* Nashville : Thomas Nelson, 2011. p. 56.

McKiddie, Eric. 2013. The Number of Hours Keller, Piper, Driscoll (and 5 Others) Spend on Sermon Prep. *Pastoraized - Becoming Better All-Around Pastors.* [Online] September 26, 2013. [Cited: June 2, 2017.] http://www.pastoralized.com/2013/09/26/the-number-of-hours-keller-piper-driscoll-and-5-others-spend-on-sermon-prep/.

Nouwen, Henri. 2016. The Way of the Heart. *The Spiritual Life: Eight Essential Titles.* San Francisco : HarperOne, 2016, p. 67.

Rainer, Thom. 2012. Five Things You Should Know About Pastors' Salaries. *Thom S. Rainer - Growing Healthy Churches. Together.* [Online] December 17, 2012. [Cited: June 1, 2017.] http://thomrainer.com/2012/12/five-things-you-should-know-about-pastors-salaries/.

Stack, Liam. 2017. Ben Carson Refers to Slaves as 'Immigrants' in First Remarks to HUD Staff. *New York Times.* [Online] March 6, 2017. [Cited: May 2, 2017.] https://www.nytimes.com/2017/03/06/us/politics/ben-carson-refers-to-slaves-as-immigrants-in-first-remarks-to-hud-staff.html?_r=0.

Stackhouse, Ian and Crisp, Oliver D., [ed.]. 2014. *Text Message: The Centrality of Scripture in Preaching.* Eugene : Pickwick, 2014. p. 137.

—. 2014. *Text Message: The Centrality of Scripture in Preaching.* Eugene : Pickwick, 2014. p. 152.

Taylor, James. 2004. *Pastors Under Pressure.* Leominster : Day One Publications, 2004. p. 64.

Wainwright, Jennifer and Hancock, Shironda. 2014. *Who's Running Your Church? The Handy Dandy Guide For Church Leaders, Administrators and Assistants.* Cleveland : Offprint, 2014. pp. 30-31, 248, 250.

—. **2014.** *Who's Running Your Church? The Handy Dandy Guide for Church Leaders, Administrators, and Assistants.* Cleveland : Offprint, 2014. pp. 173-174.

—. **2014.** *Who's Running Your Church? The Handy Dandy Guide for Church Leaders, Adminstrators, and Assistants.* Cleveland : Offprint, 2014. p. 331.

Wallace, A. J. and Dusk, R. D. 2011. *Moral Transformation: The Original Christian Paradigm of Salvation.* New Zealand : Bridgehead, 2011. pp. 227-229.

What The Bible Says About Paying Your Pastor. **Grudem, Wayne. 1981.** 2, Carol Stream : Christianity Today, 1981, CT Pastors Leadership Journal, Vol. 2.

Young, Ed. 2006. *The Creative Leader: Unleashing the Power of Your Creative Potential.* Nashville : Broadman & Holman Publishers, 2006. p. 114.

SUPPLEMENTARY READING

Myers, William H. 1991. *The Irresistible Urge to Preach.* Eugene : Wipf and Stock, 1991.